100 BEST
Cupcake
recipes

pil
Publications International, Ltd.

Front cover photography by PIL Photo Studio.
Photography on pages 7, 25, 31, 51 (top left), 55, 61, 65, 71, 75 (top left), 79, 87 and 117 by Proffitt Photography, Chicago.
Photographer: Laurie Proffitt
Photographer's Assistant: Chad Evans
Food Stylist: Carol Smoler
Assistant Food Stylist: Elaine Funk

Pictured on the front cover *(left to right):* Classic Chocolate Cupcake *(page 34),* White Chocolate Macadamia Cupcake *(page 46),* Lemon-Up Cake *(page 52),* Pink Lemonade Cupcake *(page 78)* and Angelic Cupcake *(page 110).*
Pictured on the back cover *(left to right):* Chocolate Hazelnut Cupcake *(page 6)* and Cupcake Slider *(page 86).*

Microwave Cooking: Microwave ovens vary in wattage. Use the cooking times as guidelines and check for doneness before adding more time.

Preparation/Cooking Times: Preparation times are based on the approximate amount of time required to assemble the recipe before cooking, baking, chilling or serving. These times include preparation steps such as measuring, chopping and mixing. The fact that some preparations and cooking can be done simultaneously is taken into account. Preparation of optional ingredients and serving suggestions is not included.

Contents

Cupcake Classics

Angel Almond Cupcakes

1 package DUNCAN HINES® Angel Food Cake Mix
1¼ cups water
2 teaspoons almond extract
1 container DUNCAN HINES® Wild Cherry Vanilla Frosting

1. Preheat oven to 350°F. Line 30 standard (2½-inch) muffin cups with foil or paper liners.

2. Combine cake mix, water and almond extract in large bowl. Beat at low speed with electric mixer until moistened. Beat at medium speed for 1 minute. Fill muffin cups two-thirds full. Bake at 350°F for 20 to 25 minutes or until golden brown, cracked and dry on top. Remove from muffin pans; cool completely. Frost. *Makes 30 cupcakes*

Clockwise from top left: Angel Almond Cupcakes, Chocolate Hazelnut Cupcake (page 6), Red Velvet Cupcake (page 24) and Banana Cupcakes (page 16)

Chocolate Hazelnut Cupcakes

1¾ cups all-purpose flour
1½ teaspoons baking powder
½ teaspoon salt
2 cups chocolate hazelnut spread, divided
⅓ cup butter, softened
¾ cup sugar
2 eggs
1 teaspoon vanilla
1¼ cups milk
Chopped hazelnuts (optional)

1. Preheat oven to 350°F. Line 18 standard (2½-inch) muffin cups with paper or foil baking cups.

2. Combine flour, baking powder and salt in medium bowl. Beat ⅓ cup chocolate hazelnut spread and butter in large bowl with electric mixer at medium speed until smooth. Beat in sugar until well blended. Beat in eggs and vanilla. Add flour mixture alternately with milk, beginning and ending with flour mixture. Spoon batter into prepared muffin cups, filling two-thirds full.

3. Bake 20 to 23 minutes or until cupcakes spring back when touched and toothpick inserted into centers comes out clean. Cool cupcakes in pans on wire racks 10 minutes. Remove from pans; cool completely on wire racks.

4. Frost tops of cupcakes with remaining chocolate hazelnut spread. Sprinkle with hazelnuts.   *Makes 18 cupcakes*

Chocolate Hazelnut Cupcakes

Lemon Poppy Seed Cupcakes

1½ packages (12 ounces) cream cheese, softened
1½ cups plus ⅓ cup powdered sugar, divided
  1 package (about 18 ounces) lemon cake mix, plus ingredients
     to prepare mix
  1 tablespoon poppy seeds
    Grated peel and juice of 1 lemon
    Candied violets (optional)

1. Preheat oven to 350°F. Line 18 standard (2½-inch) muffin cups with paper baking cups.

2. Beat cream cheese and ⅓ cup powdered sugar in medium bowl 1 minute or until light and fluffy.

3. Prepare cake mix according to package directions; stir in poppy seeds. Spoon 2 tablespoons batter in each prepared muffin cup. Place 2 teaspoons cream cheese mixture in center; top with 2 tablespoons batter.

4. Bake 22 to 24 minutes or until toothpick inserted into centers comes out clean. Cool cupcakes in pans on wire racks 10 minutes. Remove from pans; cool completely on wire racks.

5. Combine remaining 1½ cups powdered sugar, lemon peel and lemon juice in small bowl until well blended. Drizzle glaze over cupcakes or dip tops of cupcakes into glaze to cover completely. Top each cupcake with candied violet.   *Makes 18 cupcakes*

Lemon Poppy Seed Cupcakes

Caramel Apple Cupcakes

1 package (about 18 ounces) butter or yellow cake mix, plus ingredients to prepare mix
1 cup chopped dried apples
   Caramel Frosting (recipe follows)
   Chopped nuts (optional)

1. Preheat oven to 375°F. Line 24 standard (2½-inch) muffin cups with paper baking cups.

2. Prepare cake mix according to package directions; stir in apples. Spoon batter into prepared muffin cups, filling two-thirds full.

3. Bake 15 to 20 minutes or until toothpick inserted into centers comes out clean. Cool cupcakes in pans on wire racks 10 minutes. Remove from pans; cool completely on wire racks.

4. Prepare Caramel Frosting. Frost cupcakes; sprinkle with nuts.

Makes 24 cupcakes

Caramel Frosting

   3 tablespoons butter
   1 cup packed light brown sugar
   ½ cup evaporated milk
   ⅛ teaspoon salt
 3¾ cups powdered sugar
   ¾ teaspoon vanilla extract

Melt butter in medium saucepan. Stir in brown sugar, evaporated milk and salt; bring to a boil over medium heat, stirring constantly. Remove from heat; cool slightly. Add powdered sugar; beat until frosting reaches desired spreading consistency. Add vanilla; beat until smooth.

Makes about 2½ cups frosting

Caramel Apple Cupcakes

Peanut Butter Surprises

2 cups all-purpose flour
2 teaspoons baking powder
¼ teaspoon salt
1¾ cups sugar
½ cup (1 stick) butter, softened
¾ cup milk
1 teaspoon vanilla
3 egg whites
2 bars (3 ounces each) bittersweet chocolate candy,
melted and cooled
30 mini chocolate peanut butter cups
1 container (16 ounces) prepared chocolate frosting
3 squares (1 ounce each) white chocolate, chopped

1. Preheat oven to 350°F. Lightly grease 30 standard (2½-inch) muffin cups or line with paper baking cups.

2. Combine flour, baking powder and salt in medium bowl; mix well. Set aside. Beat sugar and butter in large bowl with electric mixer at medium speed 1 minute. Add milk and vanilla; beat at low speed 30 seconds. Gradually beat in flour mixture at medium speed 2 minutes. Add egg whites; beat 1 minute. Stir in melted chocolate.

3. Spread 1 heaping tablespoon batter into each prepared muffin cup. Place one mini peanut butter cup in center of each cupcake. Spoon 1 heaping tablespoon batter over peanut butter cup; use back of spoon to smooth out batter. (Do not fill cups more than three-fourths full.)

4. Bake 24 to 26 minutes or until puffed and edges are browned. Cool cupcakes in pans on wire racks 10 minutes. (Centers of cupcakes will sink slightly upon cooling.) Remove from pans; cool completely on wire racks. (At this point, cupcakes may be frozen up to 3 months.) Spread frosting over cooled cupcakes.

5. For white drizzle, place white chocolate in small resealable food storage bag. Microwave on HIGH 30 to 40 seconds. Turn bag over; microwave additional 30 seconds or until white chocolate is melted. Cut off tiny corner of bag; drizzle white chocolate over frosted cupcakes. Store at room temperature up to 24 hours or cover and refrigerate up to 3 days.

Makes 30 cupcakes

Peanut Butter Surprise

Cookies & Cream Cupcakes

2¼ cups all-purpose flour
1 tablespoon baking powder
½ teaspoon salt
1⅔ cups sugar
1 cup milk
½ cup (1 stick) butter, softened
2 teaspoons vanilla
3 egg whites
1 cup crushed chocolate sandwich cookies (about 10 cookies),
    plus additional for garnish
1 container (16 ounces) vanilla frosting

1. Preheat oven to 350°F. Lightly grease 24 standard (2½-inch) muffin cups or line with paper baking cups.

2. Sift flour, baking powder and salt into large bowl; stir in sugar. Add milk, butter and vanilla; beat with electric mixer at low speed 30 seconds. Beat at medium speed 2 minutes. Add egg whites; beat 2 minutes. Stir in 1 cup crushed cookies. Spoon batter into prepared muffin cups, filling two-thirds full.

3. Bake 20 to 25 minutes or until toothpick inserted into centers comes out clean. Cool cupcakes in pans on wire racks 10 minutes. Remove from pans; cool completely on wire racks.

4. Frost cupcakes; garnish with additional crushed cookies.

Makes 24 cupcakes

Banana Cupcakes

2 cups all-purpose flour
1½ cups granulated sugar
2 tablespoons packed brown sugar
2 teaspoons baking powder
½ teaspoon salt
½ teaspoon ground cinnamon
¼ teaspoon ground allspice
½ cup vegetable oil
2 eggs
¼ cup milk
1 teaspoon vanilla
2 medium mashed bananas (about 1 cup)
1 container (16 ounces) chocolate frosting
Chocolate sprinkles (optional)

1. Preheat oven to 350°F. Line 18 standard (2½-inch) muffin cups with paper baking cups.

2. Combine flour, granulated sugar, brown sugar, baking powder, salt, cinnamon and allspice in large bowl. Add oil, eggs, milk and vanilla; beat with electric mixer at medium speed 2 minutes or until well blended. Beat in bananas until well blended. Spoon batter into prepared muffin cups, filling three-fourths full.

3. Bake 25 to 30 minutes or until toothpick inserted into centers comes out clean. Cool cupcakes in pans on wire racks 10 minutes. Remove from pans; cool completely on wire racks.

4. Frost cupcakes; decorate with sprinkles. *Makes 18 cupcakes*

Banana Cupcakes

Chocolate Cherry Cupcakes

1 package (about 18 ounces) devil's food cake mix *without* pudding
    in the mix
1⅓ cups water
3 eggs
½ cup sour cream
⅓ cup vegetable oil
1 cup dried cherries
1 container (16 ounces) vanilla frosting, divided
    Green food coloring
11 maraschino cherries, stemmed and cut into halves

1. Preheat oven to 350°F. Line 22 standard (2½-inch) muffin cups with paper baking cups.

2. Beat cake mix, water, eggs, sour cream and oil in large bowl with electric mixer at low speed 30 seconds or until blended. Beat at medium speed 2 minutes or until smooth. Fold in dried cherries. Spoon batter into prepared muffin cups, filling three-fourths full.

3. Bake 20 to 24 minutes or until toothpick inserted into centers comes out clean. Cool cupcakes in pans on wire racks 10 minutes. Remove from pans; cool completely on wire racks.

4. Place ¼ cup frosting in small bowl; stir in food coloring, one drop at a time, until desired shade of green is reached.

5. Frost cupcakes with remaining vanilla frosting. Place 1 cherry half, cut side down, on each cupcake. Place green frosting in piping bag fitted with writing tip. Pipe stem onto each cupcake. Fit bag with leaf tip; pipe leaf onto each stem. *Makes 22 cupcakes*

Chocolate Cherry Cupcakes

Individual Cheesecake Cups

Crust
>   1 package DUNCAN HINES® Moist Deluxe® Classic Yellow or
>   Devil's Food Cake Mix
>   ¼ cup margarine or butter, melted

Cheese Filling
>   2 packages (8 ounces each) cream cheese, softened
>   3 eggs
>   ¾ cup sugar
>   1 teaspoon vanilla extract

Topping
>   1½ cups dairy sour cream
>   ¼ cup sugar
>   1 can (21 ounces) cherry pie filling (optional)

1. Preheat oven to 350°F. Place foil or paper liners in 24 (2½-inch) muffin cups.

2. For crust, combine cake mix and melted margarine in large bowl. Beat at low speed with electric mixer for 1 minute. (Mixture will be crumbly.) Divide mixture evenly among muffin cups. Level, but do not press.

3. For cheese filling, combine cream cheese, eggs, ¾ cup sugar and vanilla extract in medium bowl. Beat at medium speed with electric mixer until smooth. Spoon evenly into muffin cups. Bake at 350°F for 20 minutes or until set.

4. For topping, combine sour cream and ¼ cup sugar in small bowl. Spoon evenly over cheesecakes. Return to oven for 5 minutes. Cool completely. Garnish each cheesecake with cherry pie filling, if desired. Refrigerate until ready to serve.   *Makes 24 servings*

Golden Apple Cupcakes

1 package (18 to 20 ounces) yellow cake mix
1 cup MOTT'S® Chunky Apple Sauce
⅓ cup vegetable oil
3 eggs
¼ cup firmly packed light brown sugar
¼ cup chopped walnuts
½ teaspoon ground cinnamon
**   Vanilla Frosting (recipe follows)**

Heat oven to 350°F. In bowl, combine cake mix, apple sauce, oil and eggs; blend according to package directions. Spoon batter into 24 paper-lined muffin pan cups. Mix brown sugar, walnuts and cinnamon; sprinkle over prepared batter in muffin cups. Bake 20 to 25 minutes or until toothpicks inserted in centers come out clean. Cool in pan 10 minutes. Remove from pan; cool completely on wire rack. Frost cupcakes with Vanilla Frosting.

Makes 24 cupcakes

Vanilla Frosting: In large bowl, beat 1 package (8 ounces) softened cream cheese until light and creamy; blend in ¼ teaspoon vanilla extract. Beat ½ cup heavy cream until stiff; fold into cream cheese mixture. Makes about 1½ cups.

Helpful Hint

To soften cream cheese for recipes, remove it from the wrapper and place it on a medium microwavable plate. Microwave on MEDIUM (50%) for 15 to 20 seconds or until slightly softened.

Chocolate-Frosted Peanut Butter Cupcakes

1¾ cups all-purpose flour
1½ teaspoons baking powder
¼ teaspoon salt
⅓ cup butter, softened
⅓ cup peanut butter
½ cup granulated sugar
¼ cup packed brown sugar
2 eggs
1 teaspoon vanilla
1¼ cups milk
   Peanut Butter Chocolate Frosting (recipe follows)

1. Preheat oven to 350°F. Line 18 standard (2½-inch) muffin cups with foil baking cups.

2. Combine flour, baking powder and salt in medium bowl. Beat butter and peanut butter in large bowl with electric mixer at medium speed until smooth; beat in sugars until well mixed. Beat in eggs and vanilla. Add flour mixture alternately with milk, beginning and ending with flour mixture. Spoon batter into prepared muffin cups, filling two-thirds full.

3. Bake 23 to 25 minutes or until cupcakes spring back when touched and toothpick inserted into centers comes out clean. Cool cupcakes in pans on wire racks 10 minutes. Remove from pans; cool completely on wire racks.

4. Prepare Peanut Butter Chocolate Frosting. Frost each cupcake with about 1½ tablespoons frosting. *Makes 18 cupcakes*

Peanut Butter Chocolate Frosting: Beat 4 cups powdered sugar, ⅓ cup unsweetened cocoa powder, 4 tablespoons milk and 3 tablespoons creamy peanut butter in large bowl with electric mixer at low speed until smooth. Beat in additional 1 tablespoon milk if necessary to reach desired spreading consistency. Makes about 2½ cups.

Tip: If you don't have muffin pans, don't worry. Foil baking cups are sturdy enough to be used without muffin pans; simply place the baking cups on a baking sheet and fill.

Chocolate-Frosted Peanut Butter Cupcakes

Red Velvet Cupcakes

2¼ cups all-purpose flour
1 teaspoon salt
2 (1-ounce) bottles red food coloring
3 tablespoons unsweetened cocoa powder
1 cup buttermilk
1 teaspoon vanilla
1½ cups sugar
½ cup (1 stick) butter, softened
2 eggs
1 teaspoon white vinegar
1 teaspoon baking soda
1 container (16 ounces) whipped cream cheese frosting
Toasted coconut (optional)

1. Preheat oven to 350°F. Line 18 standard (2½-inch) muffin cups with paper baking cups.

2. Combine flour and salt in medium bowl. Gradually stir food coloring into cocoa in small bowl until blended and smooth. Combine buttermilk and vanilla in separate small bowl.

3. Beat sugar and butter in large bowl with electric mixer at medium speed about 4 minutes or until very light and fluffy. Add eggs, one at a time, beating well after each addition. Add cocoa mixture; beat until well blended (uniform color). Add flour mixture alternately with buttermilk mixture; beat just until blended.

4. Combine vinegar and baking soda in small bowl; gently fold into batter with spatula or spoon (do not use mixer). Spoon batter into prepared muffin cups, filling two-thirds full.

5. Bake 18 to 20 minutes or until toothpick inserted into centers comes out clean. Cool cupcakes in pans on wire racks 10 minutes. Remove from pans; cool completely on wire racks.

6. Generously spread frosting over cupcakes. Sprinkle with coconut, if desired.

Makes 18 cupcakes

Red Velvet Cupcakes

Carrot Cream Cheese Cupcakes

1 package (8 ounces) cream cheese, softened
¼ cup powdered sugar
1 package (about 18 ounces) spice cake mix, plus ingredients
   to prepare mix
2 cups grated carrots
2 tablespoons finely chopped candied ginger
1 container (16 ounces) cream cheese frosting
3 tablespoons maple syrup
   Orange peel strips (optional)

1. Preheat oven to 350°F. Spray 14 jumbo (3½-inch) muffin cups with nonstick cooking spray or line with paper or foil baking cups.

2. Beat cream cheese and powdered sugar in large bowl with electric mixer at medium speed 1 minute or until light and fluffy. Cover and refrigerate until needed.

3. Prepare cake mix according to package directions; stir in carrots and ginger. Spoon batter into prepared muffin cups, filling one-third full (about ¼ cup batter). Place 1 tablespoon cream cheese mixture in center of each cup. Top with remaining batter (do not fill cups more than two-thirds full).

4. Bake 25 to 28 minutes or until toothpick inserted into centers comes out clean. Cool cupcakes in pans on wire racks 10 minutes. Remove from pans; cool completely on wire racks.

5. Combine frosting and maple syrup until well blended. Frost cupcakes; garnish with orange peel.   *Makes 14 jumbo cupcakes*

Carrot Cream Cheese Cupcakes

Chocolate Heaven

Triple-Chocolate Cupcakes

1 package (18¼ ounces) chocolate cake mix
1 package (4 ounces) chocolate instant pudding and pie filling mix
1 container (8 ounces) sour cream
4 large eggs
½ cup vegetable oil
½ cup warm water
2 cups (12-ounce package) NESTLÉ® TOLL HOUSE® Semi-Sweet
  Chocolate Morsels
2 containers (16 ounces *each*) prepared frosting
  Assorted candy sprinkles

PREHEAT oven to 350°F. Grease or paper-line 30 muffin cups.

COMBINE cake mix, pudding mix, sour cream, eggs, vegetable oil and
water in large mixer bowl; beat on low speed just until blended. Beat on
high speed for 2 minutes. Stir in morsels. Pour into prepared muffin cups,
filling two-thirds full.

BAKE for 25 to 28 minutes or until wooden pick inserted in centers comes
out clean. Cool in pans for 10 minutes; remove to wire racks to cool
completely. Frost; decorate with candy sprinkles.   *Makes 30 cupcakes*

*Clockwise from top left: Triple-Chocolate
Cupcake, Double Malted Cupcakes (page 40),
White Chocolate Macadamia Cupcakes (page 46)
and Classic Chocolate Cupcakes (page 34)*

Decadent Brownie Cups

1 cup (2 sticks) butter
4 squares (1 ounce each) unsweetened chocolate
2 cups sugar
4 eggs
1 teaspoon vanilla
1 cup all-purpose flour
½ teaspoon salt
20 mini chocolate peanut butter cups

1. Preheat oven to 350°F. Line 20 standard (2½-inch) muffin cups with foil baking cups.

2. Heat butter and chocolate in medium saucepan over very low heat, stirring frequently, until melted and smooth. Remove pan from heat.

3. Gradually stir in sugar until well blended. Add eggs, one at a time, mixing well after each addition. Stir in vanilla. Combine flour and salt; stir into chocolate mixture. Spoon batter into prepared muffin cups, filling about two-thirds full. Place one peanut butter cup in center of each cup.

4. Bake about 18 minutes or until toothpick inserted near centers comes out clean. Serve warm or remove from pans and cool completely on wire racks.

Makes 20 cupcakes

Helpful Hint

Unsweetened and bittersweet chocolate can be stored a cool, dry place for years. Because they contain milk solids, milk chocolate and white chocolate have a much shorter shelf life and should be used within about nine months.

Decadent Brownie Cups

Celebration Chocolate Mini Cupcakes

¾ cup all-purpose flour
½ cup sugar
2 tablespoons HERSHEY'S Cocoa
½ teaspoon baking soda
¼ teaspoon salt
½ cup water
3 tablespoons vegetable oil
1½ teaspoons white vinegar
½ teaspoon vanilla extract
   Celebration Chocolate Frosting (recipe follows)

1. Heat oven to 350°F. Line 28 small (1¾-inch) muffin cups with paper or foil bake cups.

2. Stir together flour, sugar, cocoa, baking soda and salt in medium bowl. Add water, oil, vinegar and vanilla; beat with whisk or mixer on medium speed until well blended. Fill muffin cups ⅔ full with batter.

3. Bake 11 to 13 minutes or until wooden pick inserted in center comes out clean. Remove from pan to wire rack. Cool completely. Frost with Celebration Chocolate Frosting. Garnish as desired.

Makes 28 cupcakes

Note: Batter can be baked in 8 standard (2½-inch) paper-lined muffin cups. Bake at 350°F for 20 to 25 minutes.

Celebration Chocolate Frosting

1 cup powdered sugar
3 tablespoons HERSHEY'S Cocoa
3 tablespoons butter or margarine, softened
2 tablespoons water or milk
½ teaspoon vanilla extract

Stir together powdered sugar and cocoa. Beat butter and ½ cup cocoa mixture in medium bowl until blended. Add remaining cocoa mixture, water and vanilla; beat to spreading consistency.   *Makes about 1 cup frosting*

Celebration Chocolate Mini Cupcakes

32

Classic Chocolate Cupcakes

1¾ **cups all-purpose flour**
1¼ **cups sugar**
  2 **teaspoons baking powder**
  ½ **teaspoon salt**
  ¾ **cup vegetable oil**
  ¾ **cup milk**
  3 **eggs**
1½ **teaspoons vanilla**
  8 **squares (1 ounce each) semisweet baking chocolate, melted and cooled slightly**
  1 **container (16 ounces) chocolate frosting**
    Colored sprinkles or decors (optional)

1. Preheat oven to 350°F. Line 18 standard (2½-inch) muffin cups with paper baking cups.

2. Combine flour, sugar, baking powder and salt in large bowl. Add oil, milk, eggs and vanilla; beat with electric mixer at medium speed 2 minutes or until well blended. Stir in melted chocolate until well blended. Spoon batter into prepared muffin cups, filling three-fourths full.

3. Bake 25 to 30 minutes or until toothpick inserted into centers comes out clean. Cool cupcakes in pans on wire racks 10 minutes. Remove from pans; cool completely on wire racks.

4. Spread or pipe frosting over cooled cupcakes. Decorate with sprinkles.

Makes 18 cupcakes

Classic Chocolate Cupcakes

Chocolate-Raspberry Cupcakes

2 cups all-purpose flour
⅔ cup unsweetened cocoa powder
1¾ teaspoons baking soda
½ teaspoon baking powder
½ teaspoon salt
1¾ cups granulated sugar
⅔ cup vegetable shortening
1 cup cold water
2 teaspoons vanilla extract
3 large eggs
⅓ cup seedless raspberry jam
1½ cups "M&M's"® Semi-Sweet Chocolate Mini Baking Bits, divided
1 container (16 ounces) white frosting
Red food coloring

Preheat oven to 350°F. Lightly grease 24 (2¾-inch) muffin cups or line with paper or foil liners; set aside. In large bowl combine flour, cocoa powder, baking soda, baking powder and salt; stir in sugar. Beat in shortening until well combined. Gradually beat in water; stir in vanilla. Beat in eggs. Stir in raspberry jam. Divide batter evenly among prepared muffin cups. Sprinkle batter with 1 cup "M&M's"® Semi-Sweet Chocolate Mini Baking Bits. Bake 20 to 25 minutes or until toothpick inserted in centers comes out clean. Cool completely on wire racks. Combine frosting and red food coloring to make frosting pink. Spread frosting over cupcakes; decorate with remaining ½ cup" M&M's"® Semi-Sweet Chocolate Mini Baking Bits. Store in tightly covered container. *Makes 24 cupcakes*

Fudgy Mocha Cupcakes with Chocolate Coffee Ganache

1 package (about 18 ounces) devil's food cake mix *without* pudding in the mix
1 package (4-serving size) chocolate fudge instant pudding and pie filling mix
1⅓ cups very strong brewed coffee, cooled to room temperature
3 eggs
½ cup vegetable oil
6 ounces semisweet chocolate, finely chopped
½ cup whipping cream
2 teaspoons instant coffee granules
½ cup prepared white frosting

1. Preheat oven to 350°F. Line 18 standard (2½-inch) muffin cups with paper baking cups.

2. Beat cake mix, pudding mix, coffee, eggs and oil in large bowl with electric mixer at medium speed 2 minutes until well blended. Spoon batter into prepared muffin cups, filling two-thirds full.

3. Bake 22 to 24 minutes or until toothpick inserted into centers comes out clean. Cool cupcakes in pans on wire racks 10 minutes. Remove from pans; cool completely on wire racks.

4. For ganache, place chocolate in small bowl. Heat cream and instant coffee in small saucepan over medium-low heat until bubbles appear around edge of pan. Pour cream over chocolate; let stand about 2 minutes. Stir until mixture is smooth and shiny. Allow ganache to cool completely. (Ganache will be slightly runny.)

5. Dip tops of cupcakes into chocolate ganache; smooth surface. Place frosting in pastry bag fitted with writing tip. Pipe letters onto cupcakes.

Makes 18 cupcakes

Mini Turtle Cupcakes

1 package (about 21 ounces) brownie mix, plus ingredients to prepare mix
½ cup chopped pecans
1 cup prepared dark chocolate frosting
½ cup coarsely chopped pecans, toasted
12 caramels
1 to 2 tablespoons whipping cream

1. Heat oven to 350°F. Line 54 mini (1½-inch) muffin cups with paper baking cups.

2. Prepare brownie batter according to package directions; stir in chopped pecans. Spoon batter into prepared muffin cups, filling two-thirds full.

3. Bake 18 minutes or until toothpick inserted into centers comes out clean. Cool cupcakes in pans on wire racks 5 minutes. Remove from pans; cool completely on wire racks. (At this point, cupcakes may be frozen up to 3 months. Thaw at room temperature before frosting.)

4. Frost cupcakes; top with toasted pecans.

5. Combine caramels and 1 tablespoon cream in small saucepan; cook and stir over low heat until caramels are melted and mixture is smooth. Add additional 1 tablespoon cream if necessary to thin mixture. Spoon caramel evenly over cupcakes. Store at room temperature up to 24 hours or cover and refrigerate for up to 3 days.　　　　*Makes 54 mini cupcakes*

Mini Turtle Cupcakes

Double Malted Cupcakes

Cupcakes
- 2 cups all-purpose flour
- ¼ cup malted milk powder
- 2 teaspoons baking powder
- ¼ teaspoon salt
- 1¾ cups granulated sugar
- ½ cup (1 stick) butter, softened
- 1 cup milk
- 1½ teaspoons vanilla
- 3 egg whites

Frosting
- 4 ounces milk chocolate candy bar, broken into chunks
- ¼ cup (½ stick) butter
- ¼ cup whipping cream
- 1 tablespoon malted milk powder
- 1 teaspoon vanilla
- 1¾ cups powdered sugar
- 30 chocolate-covered malt ball candies

1. Preheat oven to 350°F. Line 30 standard (2½-inch) muffin cups with paper baking cups.

2. For cupcakes, combine flour, ¼ cup malted milk powder, baking powder and salt in medium bowl. Beat granulated sugar and ½ cup butter in large bowl with electric mixer at medium speed 1 minute. Add milk and 1½ teaspoons vanilla; beat at low speed 30 seconds. Gradually beat in flour mixture; beat at medium speed 2 minutes. Add egg whites; beat 1 minute. Spoon batter into prepared muffin cups, filling two-thirds full.

3. Bake 20 minutes or until golden brown and toothpick inserted into centers comes out clean. Cool cupcakes in pans on wire racks 10 minutes. (Centers will sink slightly.) Remove from pans; cool completely on wire racks.

4. For frosting, melt chocolate and ¼ cup butter in heavy saucepan over low heat, stirring frequently. Stir in cream, 1 tablespoon malted milk powder and 1 teaspoon vanilla. Gradually stir in powdered sugar. Cook 4 to 5 minutes, stirring constantly, until lumps disappear. Remove from heat. Refrigerate 20 minutes, beating every 5 minutes or until frosting is spreadable.

5. Frost cupcakes; decorate with malt ball candies.   *Makes 30 cupcakes*

Double Malted Cupcakes

Chocolate Tiramisu Cupcakes

Cupcakes
> **1 package (about 18 ounces) chocolate cake mix**
> **1¼ cups water**
> **3 eggs**
> **⅓ cup vegetable oil or melted butter**
> **2 tablespoons instant espresso powder**
> **2 tablespoons brandy (optional)**

Frosting
> **1 package (8 ounces) cream cheese or mascarpone cheese**
> **1½ to 1¾ cups powdered sugar**
> **2 tablespoons coffee-flavored liqueur (optional)**
> **1 tablespoon unsweetened cocoa powder**

1. Preheat oven to 350°F. Line 30 standard (2½-inch) muffin cups with paper baking cups.

2. For cupcakes, beat cake mix, water, eggs, oil, espresso powder and brandy, if desired, in large bowl with electric mixer at low speed 30 seconds. Beat at medium speed 2 minutes. Spoon batter into prepared muffin cups, filling two-thirds full.

3. Bake 20 to 22 minutes or until toothpick inserted into centers comes out clean. Cool cupcakes in pans on wire racks 10 minutes. Remove from pans; cool completely on wire racks. (At this point, cupcakes may be frozen up to 3 months. Thaw at room temperature before frosting.)

4. For frosting, beat cream cheese and 1½ cups powdered sugar in large bowl with electric mixer at medium speed until well blended. Add liqueur, if desired; beat until well blended. If frosting is too soft, beat in additional powdered sugar or chill until desired spreading consistency is reached.

5. Spread frosting over cooled cupcakes. Place cocoa in strainer; sprinkle over cupcakes. Store at room temperature up to 24 hours or cover and refrigerate up to 3 days. *Makes 30 cupcakes*

Miniature Brownie Cups

6 tablespoons butter or margarine, melted
¾ cup sugar
½ teaspoon vanilla extract
2 eggs
½ cup all-purpose flour
¼ cup HERSHEY'S Cocoa or HERSHEY'S SPECIAL DARK™ Cocoa
¼ teaspoon baking powder
Dash salt
¼ cup finely chopped nuts

1. Heat oven to 350°F. Line small muffin cups (1¾ inches in diameter) with paper bake cups. Stir together butter, sugar and vanilla in medium bowl. Add eggs; beat well with spoon.

2. Stir together flour, cocoa, baking powder and salt; gradually add to butter mixture, beating with spoon until well blended. Fill muffin cups ½ full with batter; sprinkle nuts over top.

3. Bake 12 to 15 minutes or until wooden pick inserted in center comes out almost clean. Cool slightly; remove brownies from pan to wire rack. Cool completely.   *Makes about 24 brownie cups*

Tip: HERSHEY'S SPECIAL DARK™ Cocoa involves a process which neutralizes the natural acidity found in cocoa powder. This results in a darker cocoa with a more mellow flavor than natural cocoa.

Prep Time: 20 minutes
Bake Time: 12 minutes
Cool Time: 25 minutes

Black Bottom Cupcakes

1 package (8 ounces) cream cheese, softened
4 eggs, divided
½ cup plus ⅓ cup granulated sugar, divided
2 cups all-purpose flour
1 cup packed brown sugar
¾ cup unsweetened cocoa powder
1 teaspoon baking powder
½ teaspoon baking soda
½ teaspoon salt
1 cup buttermilk
½ cup vegetable oil
1½ teaspoons vanilla

1. Preheat oven to 350°F. Line 20 standard (2½-inch) muffin cups with paper or foil baking cups. Beat cream cheese, 1 egg and ⅓ cup granulated sugar in small bowl until smooth and creamy; set aside.

2. Combine flour, brown sugar, cocoa, remaining ½ cup granulated sugar, baking powder, baking soda and salt in large bowl; mix well. Beat buttermilk, remaining 3 eggs, oil and vanilla in medium bowl until well blended. Add buttermilk mixture to flour mixture; beat about 2 minutes or until well blended.

3. Spoon batter into prepared muffin cups, filling about three-fourths full. Spoon heaping tablespoon cream cheese mixture over batter in each cup; gently swirl with tip of knife to marbleize.

4. Bake 20 to 25 minutes or until toothpick inserted into centers comes out clean. Cool cupcakes in pans on wire racks 5 minutes. Remove from pans; cool completely on wire racks. *Makes 20 cupcakes*

Black Bottom Cupcakes

White Chocolate Macadamia Cupcakes

**1 package (about 18 ounces) white cake mix *without* pudding in the
mix, plus ingredients to prepare mix**
**1 package (4-serving size) white chocolate instant pudding and
pie filling mix**
¾ cup chopped macadamia nuts
1 to 1½ cups flaked coconut
1 cup white chocolate chips
1 container (16 ounces) white frosting
Green food coloring (optional)

1. Preheat oven to 350°F. Line 20 standard (2½-inch) muffin cups with
paper baking cups.

2. Prepare cake mix according to package directions, beating in pudding mix
with cake mix ingredients. Fold in nuts. Spoon batter into prepared muffin
cups, filling two-thirds full.

3. Bake 18 to 20 minutes or until toothpick inserted into centers comes out
clean. Cool cupcakes in pans on wire racks 10 minutes. Remove from pans;
cool completely on wire racks.

4. Meanwhile, spread coconut evenly on ungreased baking sheet; bake
6 minutes or until light golden brown, stirring occasionally. Cool
completely.

5. Place white chocolate chips in small microwavable bowl; microwave
2 minutes on MEDIUM (50%), stirring every 30 seconds, until melted and
smooth. Cool slightly; stir into frosting. Add food coloring to frosting, if
desired, a few drops at a time, until desired shade of green is reached. Frost
cupcakes; sprinkle with toasted coconut.   *Makes 20 cupcakes*

White Chocolate Macadamia Cupcakes

Triple Chocolate PB Minis

2 packages (about 4½ ounces each) chocolate peanut butter cups*
1 package (about 18 ounces) chocolate fudge cake mix, plus
    ingredients to prepare mix
¾ cup whipping cream
1½ cups semisweet chocolate chips

*Refrigerate candy to make chopping easier.

1. Preheat oven to 350°F. Line 60 mini (1¾-inch) muffin cups with paper baking cups. Finely chop peanut butter cups; refrigerate while preparing batter.

2. Prepare cake mix according to package directions; stir in 1 cup chopped peanut butter cups. Spoon batter into prepared muffin cups, filling two-thirds full.

3. Bake about 9 minutes or until toothpick inserted into centers comes out clean. Cool cupcakes in pans on wire racks 5 minutes. Remove from pans; cool completely on wire racks.

4. Meanwhile, bring cream to a boil in small saucepan over medium-high heat. Place chocolate chips in medium bowl; pour cream over chips. Let stand 5 minutes; stir until blended and smooth. Glaze will thicken as it cools (or refrigerate glaze to thicken more quickly).

5. Dip tops of cooled cupcakes in chocolate glaze; sprinkle with remaining chopped candy.   *Makes 60 mini cupcakes*

Triple Chocolate PB Minis

Dressed to Impress

Raspberry Layer Cupcakes

2 cups all-purpose flour
2½ teaspoons baking powder
½ teaspoon salt
1 cup milk
1 teaspoon vanilla
1½ cups granulated sugar
½ cup (1 stick) butter, softened
3 eggs
1½ cups seedless raspberry jam
Powdered sugar

1. Preheat oven to 350°F. Spray 18 standard (2½-inch) muffin cups with nonstick cooking spray.

2. Combine flour, baking powder and salt in medium bowl. Combine milk and vanilla in small bowl. Beat granulated sugar and butter in large bowl with electric mixer at medium speed about 3 minutes or until creamy. Add eggs, one at a time, beating well after each addition. Add flour mixture alternately with milk mixture, beating until well blended. Spoon batter into prepared muffin cups, filling about three-fourths full.

continued on page 52

Clockwise from top left: Raspberry Layer Cupcakes, Lemon Meringue Cupcakes (page 60), Strawberry Short Cupcake (page 64) and Pumpkin Spice Cupcakes (page 54)

Raspberry Layer Cupcakes, continued

3. Bake 18 to 20 minutes or until toothpick inserted into centers comes out clean. Cool cupcakes in pans on wire racks 10 minutes. Remove from pans; cool completely on wire racks.

4. Cut cupcakes in thirds crosswise. Spread about 2 teaspoons jam over bottom layers; top with middle layers, 2 teaspoons jam and tops of cupcakes. Sprinkle with powdered sugar.   *Makes 18 cupcakes*

Lemon-Up Cakes

1 package (about 18 ounces) butter recipe white cake mix with
     pudding in the mix, plus ingredients to prepare mix
     Grated peel of 2 lemons, divided
½ cup lemon juice (2 large lemons), divided
½ cup (1 stick) butter, softened
3½ cups powdered sugar
     Yellow food coloring
1 package (9½ ounces) lemon-shaped hard candies, coarsely crushed
     or colored nonpareils

1. Preheat oven to 350°F. Spray 24 standard (2½-inch) muffin cups with nonstick cooking spray or line with paper baking cups.

2. Prepare cake mix according to package directions but use ¼ cup less water than directions call for. Stir in half of grated lemon peel and ¼ cup lemon juice. Spoon batter evenly into prepared muffin cups.

3. Bake 23 minutes or until light golden brown and toothpick inserted into centers comes out clean. Cool cupcakes in pans on wire racks 5 minutes. Remove from pans; cool completely on wire racks.

4. Beat butter in large bowl with electric mixer at medium speed until creamy. Gradually add powdered sugar. Add remaining lemon peel, ¼ cup lemon juice and several drops food coloring; beat at high speed until frosting is light and fluffy.

5. Pipe or spread frosting on cupcakes; sprinkle with candies.

Makes 24 cupcakes

Lemon-Up Cakes

Pumpkin Spice Cupcakes

1½ cups sugar
¾ cup (1½ sticks) butter, softened
3 eggs
1 can (15 ounces) solid-pack pumpkin
1 cup buttermilk
3 cups all-purpose flour
1 tablespoon baking powder
2 teaspoons ground cinnamon
1½ teaspoons baking soda
½ teaspoon salt
¼ teaspoon ground allspice
¼ teaspoon ground nutmeg
⅛ teaspoon ground ginger
    Maple Frosting (recipe follows)
    Colored decors or sugar (optional)

1. Preheat oven to 350°F. Line 24 standard (2½-inch) muffin cups with paper baking cups.

2. Beat sugar and butter in large bowl with electric mixer at medium speed 3 minutes or until light and fluffy. Add eggs, one at a time, beating well after each addition.

3. Combine pumpkin and buttermilk in medium bowl; mix well. Combine flour, baking powder, cinnamon, baking soda, salt, allspice, nutmeg and ginger in separate medium bowl. Add flour mixture to butter mixture alternately with pumpkin mixture, beating well after each addition. Spoon batter into prepared muffin cups, filling two-thirds full.

4. Bake 20 to 22 minutes or until toothpick inserted into centers comes out clean. Cool cupcakes in pans on wire racks 15 minutes. Remove from pans; cool completely on wire racks.

5. Prepare Maple Frosting; pipe or spread over cupcakes. Sprinkle with decors or sugar. *Makes 24 cupcakes*

Maple Frosting: Beat ¾ cup (1½ sticks) softened butter in large bowl with electric mixer until light and fluffy. Add 3 tablespoons maple syrup and ½ teaspoon vanilla; beat until well blended. Gradually add 3½ cups powdered sugar, beating until light and fluffy. Add 1 to 2 tablespoons milk, if necessary, to reach desired spreading consistency. Makes about 2½ cups.

Pumpkin Spice Cupcakes

Mini Tiramisu Cupcakes

1 package (about 18 ounces) yellow cake mix, plus ingredients
    to prepare mix
4 teaspoons instant espresso powder, divided
1 cup warm water
8 ounces mascarpone cheese, softened
1 cup whipping cream
3 tablespoons powdered sugar
    Grated chocolate, chocolate sprinkles or cocoa powder (optional)

1. Preheat oven to 350°F. Grease 48 mini (1¾-inch) muffin cups or line with paper baking cups.

2. Prepare cake mix according to package directions, reducing oil to 2 tablespoons. Spoon batter into prepared muffin cups, filling two-thirds full.

3. Bake 15 minutes or until toothpick inserted into centers comes out clean. Cool cupcakes in pans on wire racks 5 minutes. Remove from pans; cool completely on wire racks. Use toothpicks to poke several holes in tops of cupcakes. Leave out overnight, uncovered, to dry out.

4. At least 1 hour before serving, dissolve 3 teaspoons espresso powder in warm water. Dip tops of cupcakes in espresso; return cupcakes to wire racks.

5. Beat mascarpone in small bowl with electric mixer at medium speed until fluffy. (If mascarpone separates, continue beating until it comes back together again.)

6. Beat cream, powdered sugar and remaining 1 teaspoon espresso powder in medium bowl with electric mixer at medium speed until stiff peaks form. Fold one fourth of whipped cream mixture into mascarpone. Fold mascarpone mixture into remaining whipped cream until blended. Frost cupcakes; sprinkle with grated chocolate. Refrigerate until ready to serve.

Makes 48 mini cupcakes

Mini Tiramisu Cupcakes

Gooey Coconut Chocolate Cupcakes

**1 package (about 18 ounces) chocolate cake mix, plus ingredients
  to prepare mix**
½ cup (1 stick) butter
1 cup packed brown sugar
⅓ cup heavy cream or half-and-half
1½ cups sweetened flaked coconut
½ cup chopped pecans (optional)

1. Preheat oven to 350°F. Line 24 standard (2½-inch) muffin cups with foil or paper baking cups.

2. Prepare cake mix according to package directions. Spoon batter into prepared muffin cups, filling about half full. Bake 18 minutes or until toothpick inserted into centers comes out clean. *Do not remove cupcakes from pan.*

3. Meanwhile, melt butter in medium saucepan over low heat. Stir in brown sugar and cream until well blended and sugar is dissolved. Add coconut and pecans; mix well. Spread 2 to 3 tablespoons frosting over each cupcake.

4. Place cupcakes under preheated broiler 2 to 3 minutes or until tops begin to brown and edges bubble. Serve warm or at room temperature.

Makes 24 cupcakes

Raspberry Buckle Cupcakes

½ package (about 16 ounces) refrigerated sugar cookie dough*
½ cup all-purpose flour
¼ cup packed light brown sugar
1 teaspoon vanilla
½ cup slivered almonds
**1 package (about 18 ounces) lemon cake mix, plus ingredients to
  prepare mix**
1 can (12 ounces) raspberry pie filling

*Save remaining half package of dough for another use.

1. Preheat oven to 350°F. Line 24 standard (2½-inch) muffin cups with paper or foil baking cups.

2. For topping, combine cookie dough, flour, brown sugar and vanilla in large bowl; beat until well blended. Stir in almonds. Set aside.

3. Prepare cake mix according to package directions. Spoon batter evenly into prepared muffin cups. Place 1 tablespoon pie filling in center of each muffin cup. Bake 10 minutes.

4. Sprinkle topping evenly over partially baked cupcakes. Bake 15 minutes or until topping is browned and cupcakes are set. Cool cupcakes in pans on wire racks 10 minutes. Remove from pans; cool completely on wire racks.

Makes 24 cupcakes

Toffee Bits Cheesecake Cups

About 16 to 18 vanilla wafer cookies
3 packages (8 ounces each) cream cheese, softened
¾ cup sugar
3 eggs
1 teaspoon vanilla extract
1⅓ cups (8-ounce package) HEATH® BITS 'O BRICKLE™ Toffee Bits, divided

1. Heat oven to 350°F. Line 2½-inch muffin cups with paper bake cups; place vanilla wafer on bottom of each cup.

2. Beat cream cheese and sugar in large bowl on low speed of mixer until smooth. Beat in eggs and vanilla just until blended. Do not overbeat. Gently stir 1 cup toffee bits into batter; pour into prepared cups to ¼ inch from top.

3. Bake 20 to 25 minutes or until almost set. Remove from oven. Immediately sprinkle about ½ teaspoon toffee bits onto each cup. Cool completely in pan on wire rack. Remove from pan. Cover; refrigerate about 3 hours. Store leftover cups in refrigerator.   *Makes about 16 to 18 cups*

Lemon Meringue Cupcakes

1 package (about 18 ounces) lemon cake mix, plus ingredients to prepare mix
⅔ cup prepared lemon curd*
4 egg whites, at room temperature
6 tablespoons sugar

*Lemon curd, a thick, sweet lemon spread, is available in many supermarkets where the jams and preserves are located.

1. Preheat oven to 350°F. Line 9 jumbo (3½-inch) muffin cups with paper baking cups.

2. Prepare cake mix according to package directions. Spoon batter into prepared muffin cups, filling two-thirds full.

3. Bake 23 to 25 minutes or until toothpick inserted into centers comes out clean. Cool cupcakes in pans on wire racks 10 minutes. Remove from pans; cool on wire racks. *Increase oven temperature to 375°F.*

4. Use serrated knife to cut off tops of cupcakes even with tops of baking cups. (Do not remove paper baking cups.) Scoop out small hole in center of each cupcake with tablespoon; fill hole with generous tablespoon lemon curd. Replace cupcake tops.

5. Beat egg whites in medium bowl with electric mixer at high speed until soft peaks form. Continue beating while gradually adding sugar; beat until stiff peaks form. Pipe or spread meringue in peaks on each cupcake.

6. Place cupcakes on baking sheet. Bake 5 to 6 minutes or until peaks of meringue are golden.   *Makes 9 jumbo cupcakes*

Variation: This recipe also makes 24 standard (2½-inch) cupcakes. Line muffin cups with paper baking cups; prepare and bake cake mix according to package directions. Scoop out small hole in center of each cupcake with teaspoon and fill with generous teaspoon lemon curd. Pipe or spread about ⅓ cup meringue in peaks on each cupcake; bake as directed above.

Lemon Meringue Cupcakes

Black & Whites

**1 package (about 18 ounces) vanilla cake mix, plus ingredients
    to prepare mix**
⅔ cup semisweet chocolate chips, melted
4 ounces cream cheese, softened
1 cup prepared vanilla frosting
1 cup prepared chocolate frosting

1. Preheat oven to 350°F. Line 24 standard (2½-inch) muffin cups with paper baking cups.

2. Prepare cake mix according to package directions. Reserve half of batter (about 2½ cups) in medium bowl. Add melted chocolate and cream cheese to remaining batter; beat with electric mixer at medium speed about 2 minutes or until smooth and well blended.

3. Spoon chocolate and vanilla batters side by side into prepared muffin cups, filling about two-thirds full. (Use chocolate batter first as it is slightly thicker and easier to position on one side of muffin cups.)

4. Bake about 16 minutes or until toothpick inserted into centers comes out clean. Cool cupcakes in pans on wire racks 10 minutes. Remove from pans; cool completely on wire racks.

5. Spread vanilla frosting over half of each cupcake; spread chocolate frosting over remaining half of each cupcake.   *Makes 24 cupcakes*

Helpful Hint

To melt chocolate chips in the microwave, place the chips in a microwavable bowl and microwave on HIGH 45 seconds. Stir, then microwave for additional 10- to 20-second intervals until melted and smooth.

Strawberry Short Cupcakes

2 cups all-purpose flour
2½ teaspoons baking powder
½ teaspoon salt
1 cup milk
1 teaspoon vanilla
1½ cups plus 3 tablespoons sugar, divided
½ cup (1 stick) butter, softened
3 eggs
1½ cups cold whipping cream
2 quarts fresh strawberries, sliced

1. Preheat oven to 350°F. Spray 18 standard (2½-inch) muffin cups with nonstick cooking spray.

2. Combine flour, baking powder and salt in medium bowl. Combine milk and vanilla in measuring cup. Beat 1½ cups sugar and butter in large bowl with electric mixer at medium speed about 3 minutes or until creamy. Add eggs, one at a time, beating well after each addition. Add flour mixture alternately with milk mixture, beating until well blended. Spoon batter into prepared muffin cups, filling about three-fourths full.

3. Bake 18 to 20 minutes or until toothpick inserted into centers comes out clean. Cool cupcakes in pans on wire racks 10 minutes. Remove from pans; cool completely on wire racks.

4. Beat cream in large bowl with electric mixer at high speed until soft peaks form. Gradually add remaining 3 tablespoons sugar; beat until stiff peaks form.

5. Cut cupcakes in half crosswise. Top each bottom half with about 2 tablespoons whipped cream and strawberries. Top with top half of cupcake, whipped cream and additional strawberries.

Makes 18 cupcakes

Strawberry Short Cupcake

Boston Cream Cupcakes

**1 package (about 18 ounces) yellow cake mix, plus ingredients
to prepare mix**
¼ cup French vanilla instant pudding and pie filling mix
1 cup cold milk
1 container (16 ounces) dark chocolate frosting

1. Preheat oven to 350°F. Lightly spray 22 standard (2½-inch) muffin cups with nonstick cooking spray.

2. Prepare cake mix and bake in prepared muffin cups according to package directions for cupcakes. Cool cupcakes in pans on wire racks 10 minutes. Remove from pans; cool completely on wire racks.

3. Meanwhile, whisk pudding mix and milk until well blended. Cover and refrigerate until needed.

4. Gently poke small hole in bottom of each cupcake with tip of knife or toothpick. Place pudding in pastry bag fitted with small round pastry tip.* Place tip inside holes in cupcakes; gently squeeze bag to fill cupcakes with pudding.

5. Place frosting in medium microwavable bowl. Microwave on HIGH 30 seconds; stir. Frost tops of cupcakes.   *Makes 22 cupcakes*

*Or use a plastic squeeze bottle with a narrow dispensing tip.

Cappuccino Cupcakes

1 package (about 18 ounces) dark chocolate cake mix
1⅓ cups strong brewed or instant coffee, at room temperature
3 eggs
⅓ cup vegetable oil or melted butter
1 container (16 ounces) vanilla frosting
2 tablespoons coffee liqueur
Additional coffee liqueur (optional)
Grated chocolate*
Chocolate-covered coffee beans (optional)

*Grate a 1½-ounce milk, dark or espresso chocolate candy bar on the large holes of a grater.

1. Preheat oven to 350°F. Line 24 standard (2½-inch) muffin cups with foil or paper baking cups.

2. Beat cake mix, coffee, eggs and oil with electric mixer at low speed 30 seconds. Beat at medium speed 2 minutes. Spoon batter into prepared muffin cups, filling two-thirds full.

3. Bake 18 to 20 minutes or until toothpick inserted into centers comes out clean. Cool cupcakes in pans on wire racks 10 minutes. Remove from pans; cool completely on wire racks.

4. Combine frosting and 2 tablespoons liqueur in small bowl; mix well. Poke about 10 holes in each cupcake with toothpick. Pour 1 to 2 teaspoons liqueur over top of each cupcake. Frost cupcakes and sprinkle with grated chocolate. Garnish with chocolate-covered coffee beans.

Makes 24 cupcakes

His and Her Cupcakes

    1 package (about 18 ounces) cake mix, any flavor, plus ingredients
        to prepare mix
    1 container (16 ounces) vanilla frosting
    3 rolls (¾ ounce each) chewy fruit roll-ups, cut into 4×2⅜-inch strips
   12 pieces striped fruit gum
      Red food coloring
   24 vanilla wafer cookies
      Assorted candies and colored sprinkles

1. Preheat oven to 350°F. Line 24 standard (2½-inch) muffin cups with paper baking cups or spray with nonstick cooking spray.

2. Prepare cake mix and bake in prepared muffin cups according to package directions for cupcakes. Cool cupcakes in pans on wire racks 15 minutes. Remove from pans; cool completely on wire racks.

3. For "His" cupcakes, frost 12 cupcakes. Place one strip fruit snack, shaped into circle, on each frosted cupcake to form shirt collar. Cut gum into tie shapes and place on cupcakes in front of fruit snack.

4. For "Her" cupcakes, tint remaining frosting pink with food coloring. Frost remaining cupcakes with tinted frosting. Use small amount of frosting to sandwich two vanilla wafer cookies together. Repeat with remaining cookies. Frost cookie sandwiches with additional pink frosting. Top each cupcake with cookie sandwich, placing slightly off-center to form crown of hat. Decorate hats with fruit snacks and candies. *Makes 24 cupcakes*

Mini Cocoa Cupcake Kabobs

1 cup sugar
1 cup all-purpose flour
⅓ cup HERSHEY'S Cocoa
¾ teaspoon baking powder
¾ teaspoon baking soda
½ teaspoon salt
1 egg
½ cup milk
¼ cup vegetable oil
1 teaspoon vanilla extract
½ cup boiling water
    Lickety-Split Cocoa Frosting (recipe follows)
    Jelly beans or sugar nonpareils and/or decorating frosting
    Marshmallows
    Strawberries
    Wooden or metal skewers

1. Heat oven to 350°F. Spray small muffin cups (1¾ inches in diameter) with vegetable cooking spray.

2. Stir together sugar, flour, cocoa, baking powder, baking soda and salt in medium bowl. Add egg, milk, oil and vanilla; beat on medium speed of mixer 2 minutes. Stir in boiling water (batter will be thin). Fill muffin cups about ⅔ full with batter.

3. Bake 10 minutes or until wooden pick inserted in center comes out clean. Cool slightly; remove from pans to wire racks. Cool completely. Frost with Lickety-Split Cocoa Frosting. Garnish with jelly beans, nonpareils and/or white frosting piped onto cupcake. Alternate cupcakes, marshmallows and strawberries on skewers.   *Makes about 4 dozen cupcakes*

Lickety-Split Cocoa Frosting: Beat 3 tablespoons softened butter or margarine in small bowl until creamy. Add 1¼ cups powdered sugar, ¼ cup HERSHEY'S Cocoa, 2 to 3 tablespoons milk and ½ teaspoon vanilla extract until smooth and of desired consistency. Makes about 1 cup frosting

Note: Number of kabobs will be determined by length of skewer used and number of cupcakes, marshmallows and strawberries placed on each skewer.

Mini Cocoa Cupcake Kabobs

Almond Raspberry Cream Cupcakes

2¾ cups all-purpose flour
2½ teaspoons baking powder
 ¾ teaspoon salt
1¾ cups granulated sugar
 ¾ cup (1½ sticks) butter, softened
 1 teaspoon almond extract
 1 teaspoon vanilla
 4 eggs
 2 egg yolks
1½ cups milk
    Raspberry Cream (recipe follows)
    Powdered sugar

1. Preheat oven to 350°F. Line 18 standard (2½-inch) muffin cups with paper baking cups.

2. Combine flour, baking powder and salt in medium bowl. Beat granulated sugar, butter, almond extract and vanilla in large bowl with electric mixer at medium speed 4 minutes or until light and fluffy. Add eggs and egg yolks, one at a time, beating well after each addition. Alternately add flour mixture and milk, beating well after each addition. Spoon batter into prepared muffin cups, filling three-fourths full.

3. Bake 20 to 22 minutes or until toothpick inserted into centers comes out clean. Cool cupcakes in pans on wire racks 15 minutes. Remove from pans; cool completely on wire racks.

4. Prepare Raspberry Cream. Cut tops off cupcakes; spread with Raspberry Cream. Replace cupcake tops; sprinkle with powdered sugar.

Makes 18 cupcakes

Raspberry Cream: Beat 1 cup cold whipping cream and ¼ cup powdered sugar in large bowl with electric mixer at high speed 5 minutes or until cream is thickened and almost stiff. Place 1 pint fresh raspberries in small bowl; mash lightly with fork. Gently fold raspberries into whipped cream mixture until well blended and evenly colored. Makes about 3 cups.

Almond Raspberry Cream Cupcakes

Iced Coffee Cupcakes

**1 package (about 18 ounces) chocolate fudge cake mix *without*
    pudding in the mix**
**1 package (4-serving size) chocolate instant pudding and
    pie filling mix**
1⅓ cups brewed coffee, cooled to room temperature
3 eggs
½ cup vegetable oil
1 teaspoon vanilla
    Half gallon mocha almond fudge or coffee ice cream, softened
1 bottle (7¼ ounces) quick-hardening chocolate shell dessert topping
½ cup pecan pieces, toasted

1. Preheat oven to 350°F. Line 20 standard (2½-inch) muffin cups with foil
or paper baking cups or spray with nonstick cooking spray.

2. Beat cake mix, pudding mix, coffee, eggs, oil and vanilla in large bowl
with electric mixer at low speed 30 seconds. Beat at medium speed about
2 minutes or until well blended and fluffy. Spoon batter into prepared
muffin cups, filling three-fourths full.

3. Bake 15 to 20 minutes or until toothpick inserted into centers comes out
clean. Cool cupcakes in pans on wire racks 10 minutes. Remove from pans;
cool completely on wire racks.

4. Remove 1 tablespoon cake from center of one cupcake. Fill hole with
2 to 3 tablespoons ice cream, mounding slightly. Spoon about 1 tablespoon
dessert topping over ice cream; quickly sprinkle with pecans before topping
hardens. Place in freezer until ready to serve. Repeat with remaining
cupcakes, ice cream, topping and pecans.   *Makes 20 cupcakes*

Iced Coffee Cupcakes

Especially for Kids

Quick Cookie Cupcakes

**1 package (about 16 ounces) refrigerated chocolate chip cookie
    dough (24 count)**
1 cup chocolate frosting
    Colored decors

1. Preheat oven to 350°F. Line 24 mini (1¾-inch) muffin cups with paper baking cups.

2. Break dough into 24 pieces along score lines. Roll each piece into ball; place in prepared muffin cups. Bake 10 to 12 minutes or until golden brown. Cool cupcakes in pans on wire racks 5 minutes. Remove from pans; cool on wire racks.

3. Spread frosting over each cupcake. Sprinkle with decors.

Makes 24 mini cupcakes

*Clockwise from top left: Quick Cookie Cupcake,
Pink Lemonade Cupcakes (page 78),
Cupcake Slider (page 86) and
Miss Pinky the Pig Cupcakes (page 102)*

Marshmallow Fudge Sundae Cupcakes

1 package (about 18 ounces) chocolate cake mix, plus ingredients
    to prepare mix
2 packages (4 ounces each) waffle bowls
40 large marshmallows
1 jar (8 ounces) hot fudge topping
1¼ cups whipped topping
    Colored sprinkles
20 maraschino cherries, drained

1. Preheat oven to 350°F. Lightly spray 20 standard (2½-inch) muffin cups with nonstick cooking spray.

2. Prepare cake mix according to package directions. Spoon batter into prepared muffin cups, filling two-thirds full.

3. Bake 20 minutes or until toothpick inserted into centers comes out clean. Cool cupcakes in pans on wire racks about 10 minutes.

4. Remove cupcakes from pans; place one cupcake in each waffle bowl. Place waffle bowls on baking sheets. Top each sundae with 2 marshmallows; return to oven 2 minutes or until marshmallows are slightly softened.

5. Remove lid from fudge topping; heat in microwave on HIGH 10 seconds or until softened. Top each sundae with 2 teaspoons fudge topping, 1 tablespoon whipped topping, sprinkles and a cherry.

Makes 20 sundaes

Porcupine Cupcakes

1 package DUNCAN HINES® Moist Deluxe® Cake Mix (any flavor)
1 container DUNCAN HINES® Chocolate Frosting
    Sliced almonds

1. Preheat oven to 350°F. Place 2½-inch paper liners in 24 muffin cups.

2. Prepare, bake and cool cupcakes following package directions for basic recipe. Frost cupcakes with Chocolate frosting. Place sliced almonds upright on each cupcake to decorate as a "porcupine."   *Makes 24 cupcakes*

Tip: Slivered almonds can be used in place of sliced almonds.

Marshmallow Fudge Sundae Cupcakes

Pink Lemonade Cupcakes

1 package (about 18 ounces) white cake mix *without* pudding in the mix
1 cup water
3 egg whites
⅓ cup plus ¼ cup frozen pink lemonade concentrate, thawed, divided
2 tablespoons vegetable oil
5 to 8 drops red food coloring, divided
4 cups sifted powdered sugar
⅓ cup butter, softened
   Lemon slice candies (optional)

1. Preheat oven to 350°F. Line 24 standard (2½-inch) muffin cups with paper baking cups.

2. Beat cake mix, water, egg whites, ⅓ cup lemonade concentrate, oil and 4 to 6 drops food coloring in large bowl with electric mixer at medium speed 2 minutes. Spoon batter evenly into prepared muffin cups.

3. Bake 18 to 22 minutes or until toothpick inserted into centers comes out clean. Cool cupcakes in pans on wire racks 5 minutes. Remove from pans; cool completely on wire racks.

4. Beat powdered sugar, butter and remaining ¼ cup lemonade concentrate in medium bowl with electric mixer at medium speed until smooth. Beat in remaining food coloring until desired shade of pink is reached. Frost cupcakes. Garnish with candies and straws, if desired.

Makes 24 cupcakes

Pink Lemonade Cupcakes

Butterfly Cupcakes

**1 package (about 18 ounces) cake mix, any flavor, plus ingredients
to prepare mix**
1 container (16 ounces) white frosting
Blue and green food coloring
Assorted candies and colored sugar
Red licorice strings, cut into 4-inch pieces

1. Preheat oven to 350°F. Lightly spray 24 standard (2½-inch) muffin cups
with nonstick cooking spray.

2. Prepare cake mix according to package directions. Spoon batter into
prepared muffin cups, filling two-thirds full.

3. Bake about 20 minutes or until toothpick inserted into centers comes
out clean. Cool cupcakes in pans on wire racks 10 minutes. Remove from
pans; cool completely on wire racks.

4. Divide frosting between 2 small bowls. Add one color food coloring to
each bowl, one drop at a time, until desired shades of blue and green are
reached.

5. Cut cupcakes in half vertically. Place halves together, cut sides out, to
resemble butterfly wings. Frost cupcakes and decorate with candies and
colored sugar as desired. Snip each end of licorice string pieces to form
antennae; place down center of each butterfly.   *Makes 24 cupcakes*

Butterfly Cupcakes

Banana Split Cupcakes

  1 package (about 18 ounces) yellow cake mix, divided
  1 cup water
  1 cup mashed ripe bananas
  3 eggs
  1 cup chopped drained maraschino cherries
1½ cups mini semisweet chocolate chips, divided
1½ cups prepared vanilla frosting
  1 cup marshmallow creme
  1 teaspoon shortening
 30 whole maraschino cherries, drained and patted dry

1. Preheat oven to 350°F. Line 30 standard (2½-inch) muffin cups with paper baking cups.

2. Reserve 2 tablespoons cake mix. Beat remaining cake mix, water, bananas and eggs in large bowl with electric mixer at low speed about 30 seconds or until moistened. Beat at medium speed 2 minutes. Combine chopped cherries and reserved cake mix in small bowl. Stir chopped cherry mixture and 1 cup chocolate chips into batter. Spoon batter into prepared muffin cups, filling two-thirds full.

3. Bake 15 to 20 minutes or until toothpick inserted into centers comes out clean. Cool cupcakes in pans on wire racks 10 minutes. Remove from pans; cool completely on wire racks.

4. Combine frosting and marshmallow creme in medium bowl until well blended. Frost cupcakes.

5. Combine remaining ½ cup chocolate chips and shortening in small microwavable bowl. Microwave on MEDIUM (50%) 30 to 45 seconds, stirring after 30 seconds, or until melted and smooth. Drizzle chocolate mixture over cupcakes. Place one whole cherry on each cupcake.

Makes 30 cupcakes

Note: If desired, omit chocolate drizzle and top cupcakes with colored sprinkles.

Banana Split Cupcakes

Peanut Butter & Milk Chocolate Cupcakes

1 package (about 18 ounces) butter recipe yellow cake mix with pudding in the mix, plus ingredients to prepare mix
½ cup creamy peanut butter
¼ cup (½ stick) butter
2 bars (3½ ounces each) good-quality milk chocolate, broken into small pieces
¼ cup (½ stick) butter, cut into small chunks
¼ cup whipping cream
Dash salt
Peanut butter chips (optional)

1. Preheat oven to 350°F. Line 24 standard (2½-inch) muffin cups with paper baking cups.

2. Prepare cake mix according to package directions with ½ cup peanut butter and ¼ cup butter (instead of ½ cup butter called for in directions). Spoon batter evenly into prepared muffin cups.

3. Bake 24 to 26 minutes or until light golden brown and toothpick inserted into centers comes out clean. Cool cupcakes in pans on wire racks 5 minutes. Remove from pans; cool completely on wire racks.

4. Combine chocolate, remaining ¼ cup butter, cream and salt in small, heavy saucepan. Heat over very low heat, stirring constantly, just until butter and chocolate are melted. Mixture should be warm, not hot. Immediately spoon about 1 tablespoon chocolate glaze over each cupcake, spreading to cover top. Sprinkle with peanut butter chips.   *Makes 24 cupcakes*

"Go Fly a Kite" Cupcakes

1⅔ cups all-purpose flour
½ cup unsweetened cocoa powder
1 teaspoon baking powder
½ teaspoon baking soda
¼ teaspoon salt
1¾ cups granulated sugar
¼ cup firmly packed light brown sugar
½ cup vegetable shortening
1 cup buttermilk
3 large eggs
2 tablespoons vegetable oil
¾ teaspoon vanilla extract
1½ cups "M&M's"® Chocolate Mini Baking Bits, divided
24 graham cracker squares
1 container (16 ounces) white frosting
Assorted food colorings

Preheat oven to 350°F. Lightly grease 24 (2¾-inch) muffin cups or line with foil or paper liners; set aside. In large bowl combine flour, cocoa powder, baking powder, baking soda and salt; stir in sugars. Beat in shortening until well combined. Beat in buttermilk, eggs, oil and vanilla. Divide batter among prepared muffin cups. Sprinkle 1 teaspoon "M&M's"® Chocolate Mini Baking Bits over batter in each muffin cup. Bake 20 to 25 minutes or until toothpick inserted in centers comes out clean. Cool completely on wire racks. Using serrated knife and back and forth sawing motion, gently cut graham crackers into kite shapes. (Do not press down on cracker while cutting.) Reserve 1 cup frosting. Tint remaining frosting desired color. Frost graham crackers and decorate with "M&M's"® Chocolate Mini Baking Bits. Tint reserved frosting sky blue; frost cupcakes. Place small blob frosting at one edge of cupcake; stand kites in frosting on cupcakes. Make kite tails with "M&M's"® Chocolate Mini Baking Bits. Store in tightly covered container.   *Makes 24 cupcakes*

Cupcake Sliders

2 cups all-purpose flour
2½ teaspoons baking powder
½ teaspoon salt
1 cup milk
½ teaspoon vanilla
1½ cups sugar
1 cup (1 stick) butter, softened
3 eggs
1¼ cups chocolate hazelnut spread or milk chocolate frosting
    Colored decors (optional)

1. Preheat oven to 350°F. Spray 18 standard (2½-inch) muffin cups with nonstick cooking spray.

2. Combine flour, baking powder and salt in medium bowl. Combine milk and vanilla in measuring cup. Beat sugar and butter in large bowl with electric mixer at medium speed 3 minutes or until creamy. Add eggs, one at a time, beating well after each addition. Add flour mixture alternately with milk mixture, beating until well blended. Spoon batter into prepared muffin cups, filling about three-fourths full.

3. Bake 18 to 20 minutes or until toothpick inserted into centers comes out clean. Cool cupcakes in pans on wire racks 10 minutes. Remove from pans; cool completely on wire racks.

4. Cut off edges of cupcakes to form squares. Cut cupcakes in half crosswise. Spread each bottom half with about 1 tablespoon chocolate hazelnut spread; sprinkle with decors. Replace tops of cupcakes.

Makes 18 cupcakes

Cupcake Sliders

Pupcakes

**1 package (about 18 ounces) chocolate cake mix, plus ingredients
    to prepare mix**
½ cup (1 stick) butter, softened
4 cups powdered sugar
¼ to ½ cup half-and-half or milk
    Red and yellow fruit roll-ups
    Candy-coated chocolate pieces
    Assorted colored jelly beans

1. Preheat oven to 350°F. Line 24 standard (2½-inch) muffin cups with paper baking cups.

2. Prepare cake mix and bake in prepared muffin cups according to package directions for cupcakes. Cool cupcakes in pans on wire racks 15 minutes. Remove from pans; cool completely on wire racks.

3. Beat butter in large bowl with electric mixer until creamy. Gradually add powdered sugar, scraping down side of bowl occasionally. (Frosting will be stiff.) Gradually add half-and-half until frosting reaches desired consistency. Frost cupcakes.

4. Cut out ear and tongue shapes from fruit roll-ups with scissors; press into frosting. Add chocolate pieces and jelly beans to create eyes and noses.

Makes 24 cupcakes

Pupcakes

Rabbit Power Brownie Cupcakes

1¼ cups sugar
  1 cup all-purpose flour
  ½ cup unsweetened cocoa powder
  ½ teaspoon baking powder
  ½ teaspoon baking soda
  ¼ teaspoon salt
  ⅔ cup vegetable oil
  ½ cup shredded carrot (about 1 medium carrot)
  2 eggs
  ¼ cup milk
  1 teaspoon vanilla
  1 container (16 ounces) chocolate frosting
    Colored sprinkles (optional)

1. Preheat oven to 350°F. Line 16 standard (2½-inch) muffin cups with paper or foil baking cups.

2. Combine sugar, flour, cocoa, baking powder, baking soda and salt in large bowl. Add oil, carrot, eggs, milk and vanilla; beat with electric mixer at low speed until blended. Beat at medium speed 2 minutes. Spoon batter into prepared muffin cups, filling about two-thirds full.

3. Bake about 15 minutes or until toothpick inserted into centers comes out clean. Cool cupcakes in pans on wire racks 5 minutes. Remove from pans; cool completely on wire racks.

4. Frost cupcakes with chocolate frosting. Decorate with sprinkles.

Makes 16 cupcakes

Rabbit Power Brownie Cupcakes

Captivating Caterpillar Cupcakes

1 package DUNCAN HINES® Moist Deluxe® White Cake Mix
3 egg whites
1⅓ cups water
2 tablespoons vegetable oil
½ cup star decors, divided
1 container DUNCAN HINES® Vanilla Frosting
Green food coloring
6 chocolate sandwich cookies, finely crushed (see Hint)
½ cup candy-coated chocolate pieces
⅓ cup assorted jelly beans
Assorted nonpareil decors

1. Preheat oven to 350°F. Line 24 standard (2½-inch) muffin cups with paper liners.

2. Combine cake mix, egg whites, water and oil in large bowl. Beat at low speed with electric mixer until moistened. Beat at medium speed 2 minutes. Fold in ⅓ cup star decors. Fill paper liners about half full. Bake at 350°F for 18 to 23 minutes or until toothpick inserted in center comes out clean. Cool in pans 5 minutes. Remove to cooling racks. Cool completely.

3. Tint Vanilla frosting with green food coloring. Frost one cupcake. Sprinkle ½ teaspoon chocolate cookie crumbs on frosting. Arrange 4 candy-coated chocolate pieces to form caterpillar body. Place jelly bean at one end to form head. Attach remaining star and nonpareil decors with dots of frosting to form eyes. Repeat with remaining cupcakes.

Makes 24 cupcakes

Helpful Hint

To finely crush chocolate sandwich cookies,
place cookies in resealable plastic bag.
Remove excess air from bag; seal. Press rolling pin
on top of cookies to break into pieces. Continue
pressing until evenly crushed.

Chocolate Malts

Cupcakes
  1¾ **cups cake flour**
  1¼ **cups sugar, divided**
   ¾ **teaspoon baking soda**
   ½ **teaspoon salt**
   2 **eggs**
   ⅓ **cup vegetable oil**
   1 **cup buttermilk**
   ¼ **cup chocolate malted milk powder**
   1 **teaspoon vanilla**

Marshmallow Frosting
   1 **cup thawed frozen whipped topping**
   ½ **cup marshmallow creme**
     Chopped malted milk balls
     Additional chocolate malted milk powder

1. Preheat oven to 350°F. Grease and flour 12 standard (2½-inch) muffin cups or line with paper baking cups.

2. Sift flour, ¾ cup sugar, baking soda and salt into medium bowl. Beat eggs and remaining ½ cup sugar in large bowl with electric mixer at medium-high speed 3 minutes or until light and glossy. Add one third of flour mixture; beat at low speed until thick. Add oil; beat until smooth.

3. Combine buttermilk, malted milk powder and vanilla in small bowl; stir until powder is dissolved. Add one third of buttermilk mixture to batter; beat until smooth. Add remaining flour mixture alternately with remaining buttermilk mixture, beating well after each addition. Spoon batter evenly into prepared muffin cups.

4. Bake about 25 minutes or until toothpick inserted into centers comes out clean. Cool cupcakes in pan on wire rack 15 minutes. Remove from pan; cool completely on wire rack.

5. Stir whipped topping and marshmallow creme in medium bowl until well blended and smooth. Spread frosting over cupcakes. Sprinkle with malted milk balls; dust with additional malted milk powder.

Makes 12 cupcakes

Ice Cream Cone Cupcakes

**1 package (about 18 ounces) white cake mix, plus ingredients
    to prepare mix**
2 tablespoons nonpareils
24 flat-bottomed ice cream cones
   Prepared vanilla and chocolate frostings
   Additional nonpareils and decors

1. Preheat oven to 350°F.

2. Prepare cake mix according to package directions; stir in nonpareils. Stand ice cream cones in 13×9-inch baking pan or muffin cups. Spoon ¼ cup batter into each cone.

3. Bake about 20 minutes or until toothpick inserted into centers comes out clean. Cool cupcakes completely on wire racks.

4. Frost cupcakes and decorate as desired.   *Makes 24 cupcakes*

Note: These cupcakes are best served the day they are prepared. If it is necessary to store them, cover loosely.

Mini Doughnut Cupcakes

  1 cup sugar
1½ teaspoons ground cinnamon
  **1 package (about 18 ounces) yellow or white cake mix, plus
     ingredients to prepare mix**
  1 tablespoon ground nutmeg

1. Preheat oven to 350°F. Grease and flour 48 mini (1¾-inch) muffin cups. Combine sugar and cinnamon in small bowl; set aside.

2. Prepare cake mix according to package directions; stir in nutmeg. Spoon batter into prepared muffin cups, filling two-thirds full.

3. Bake about 12 minutes or until lightly browned and toothpick inserted into centers comes out clean.

4. Remove cupcakes from pans. Roll warm cupcakes in sugar mixture until completely coated.   *Makes 48 mini cupcakes*

Ice Cream Cone Cupcakes

P.B. Chips Brownie Cups

1 cup (2 sticks) butter or margarine
2 cups sugar
2 teaspoons vanilla extract
4 eggs
¾ cup HERSHEY'S Cocoa or HERSHEY'S SPECIAL DARK™ Cocoa
1¾ cups all-purpose flour
½ teaspoon baking powder
½ teaspoon salt
1⅔ cups (10-ounce package) REESE'S® Peanut Butter Chips, divided

1. Heat oven to 350°F. Line 18 muffin cups (2½ inches in diameter) with paper or foil bake cups.

2. Place butter in large microwave-safe bowl. Microwave at HIGH (100%) 1 to 1½ minutes or until melted. Stir in sugar and vanilla. Add eggs; beat well. Add cocoa; beat until well blended. Add flour, baking powder and salt; beat well. Stir in 1⅓ cups peanut butter chips. Divide batter evenly among muffin cups.

3. Bake 25 to 30 minutes or until surface is firm; remove from oven. Immediately sprinkle remaining ⅓ cup peanut butter chips over muffin tops, pressing in slightly. Cool completely in pans on wire rack.

Makes 1½ dozen brownie cups

Cookie Sundae Cups

1 package (about 16 ounces) refrigerated chocolate chip cookie dough
6 cups ice cream, any flavor (1½ quarts)
Ice cream topping, whipped cream and colored sprinkles

1. Preheat oven to 350°F. Lightly grease 18 standard (2½-inch) muffin cups.

2. Let dough stand at room temperature about 15 minutes. Shape dough into 18 balls; press onto bottoms and up sides of prepared muffin cups.

3. Bake 14 to 18 minutes or until golden brown. Cool cookie cups in pans on wire racks 10 minutes. Remove from pans; cool completely on wire racks.

4. Place ⅓ cup ice cream in each cookie cup. Drizzle with topping; top with whipped cream and sprinkles.

Makes 18 sundae cups

P.B. Chips Brownie Cups

Tropical Luau Cupcakes

2 cans (8 ounces each) crushed pineapple in juice
1 package (about 18 ounces) yellow cake mix *without* pudding
in the mix
1 package (4-serving size) banana cream instant pudding and
pie filling mix
4 eggs
⅓ cup vegetable oil
¼ teaspoon ground nutmeg
1 container (12 ounces) whipped vanilla frosting
¾ cup flaked coconut, toasted*
3 to 4 medium kiwi
30 (2½-inch) pretzel sticks

*To toast coconut, spread evenly on ungreased baking sheet. Toast in preheated 350°F oven 5 to 7 minutes, stirring occasionally, until light golden brown.

1. Preheat oven to 350°F. Line 30 standard (2½-inch) muffin cups with paper baking cups. Drain pineapple, reserving juice. Set pineapple aside.

2. Beat cake mix, pudding mix, eggs, reserved pineapple juice, oil and nutmeg in large bowl with electric mixer at low speed 1 minute or until blended. Beat at medium speed 1 to 2 minutes or until smooth. Fold in pineapple. Spoon batter into prepared muffin cups, filling two-thirds full.

3. Bake 20 minutes or until toothpick inserted into centers comes out clean. Cool cupcakes in pans on wire racks 5 minutes. Remove from pans; cool completely on wire racks.

4. Frost tops of cupcakes with frosting; sprinkle with coconut. For palm trees,* peel kiwi and cut into ⅛-inch-thick slices. Create palm fronds by cutting each slice at ⅜-inch intervals, cutting from outside edge toward center. (Leave about ¾- to 1-inch circle uncut in center of each slice). For palm tree trunk, push pretzel stick into, but not through, center of each kiwi slice. Push other end of pretzel into top of each cupcake.

Makes 30 cupcakes

*Palm tree decorations can be made up to 1 hour before serving.

S'More Cups

    1 package (about 16 ounces) refrigerated chocolate chip cookie dough
    1 cup graham cracker crumbs
1⅔ cups semisweet chocolate chips
    1 cup whipping cream
    1 package (10 ounces) mini marshmallows
  18 bear-shaped graham crackers

1. Preheat oven to 350°F. Lightly grease 18 standard (2½-inch) muffin cups or line with paper or foil baking cups. Let dough stand at room temperature about 15 minutes.

2. Combine dough and graham cracker crumbs in large bowl; beat until well blended. Shape dough into 18 balls; press onto bottoms and up sides of prepared muffin cups.

3. Bake 12 to 15 minutes or until set. Remove from oven; gently press down center of each cookie cup with back of teaspoon. Cool cups in pans on wire racks 10 minutes. Remove from pans; cool completely on wire racks.

4. Place chocolate chips in large bowl. Place cream in small saucepan; bring to a boil over medium heat. Pour cream over chocolate chips; stir until chocolate is melted and mixture is smooth. Cool 5 minutes. Meanwhile, preheat broiler.

5. Place cookie cups on ungreased cookie sheet. Divide chocolate mixture evenly among cookie cups; top each cup with 7 marshmallows. Broil cookie cups 20 to 30 seconds or until marshmallows are golden brown. Top with graham crackers.   *Makes 18 cups*

Lazy Daisy Cupcakes

    1 package (about 18 ounces) yellow cake mix, plus ingredients
        to prepare mix
    Yellow food coloring
    1 container (16 ounces) vanilla frosting
  30 large marshmallows
  24 small gumdrops

1. Line 24 standard (2½-inch) muffin cups with paper baking cups or spray with nonstick cooking spray.

2. Prepare cake mix and bake in prepared muffin cups according to package directions for cupcakes. Cool cupcakes in pans on wire racks 15 minutes. Remove from pans; cool completely on wire racks.

3. Add food coloring to frosting, a few drops at a time, until desired shade of yellow is reached. Frost cupcakes.

4. Cut each marshmallow crosswise into 4 pieces with scissors. Stretch pieces into petal shapes; place 5 pieces on each cupcake to form flower. Place gumdrop in center of each flower.   *Makes 24 cupcakes*

Berry Surprise Cupcakes

1 package DUNCAN HINES® Moist Deluxe® White Cake Mix
3 egg whites
1⅓ cups water
2 tablespoons vegetable oil
3 sheets (0.5 ounce each) strawberry chewy fruit snacks
1 container DUNCAN HINES® Vanilla Frosting
2 pouches (0.9 ounce each) chewy fruit snack shapes, for garnish
**   (optional)**

1. Preheat oven to 350°F. Line 24 standard (2½-inch) muffin cups with paper liners.

2. Combine cake mix, egg whites, water and oil in large bowl. Beat at low speed with electric mixer until moistened. Beat at medium speed 2 minutes. Fill each liner half full with batter.

3. Cut three fruit snack sheets into 9 equal pieces. (You will have 3 extra squares.) Place each fruit snack piece on top of batter in each cup. Pour remaining batter equally over each. Bake at 350°F for 18 to 23 minutes or until toothpick inserted in center comes out clean. Cool in pans 5 minutes. Remove to cooling racks. Cool completely. Frost cupcakes with Vanilla frosting. Decorate with fruit snack shapes, if desired.

Makes 24 cupcakes

Variation: To make a Berry Surprise Cake, prepare cake following package directions. Pour half the batter into prepared 13×9×2-inch pan. Place 4 fruit snack sheets evenly on top. Pour remaining batter over all. Bake and cool as directed on package. Frost and decorate as directed.

Miss Pinky the Pig Cupcakes

2 jars (10 ounces each) maraschino cherries, well drained
1 package (about 18 ounces) white cake mix *without* pudding in the mix
1 cup sour cream
½ cup vegetable oil
3 egg whites
¼ cup water
½ teaspoon almond extract
    Red food coloring
1 container (16 ounces) cream cheese frosting
48 small gumdrops
    Mini candy-coated chocolate pieces, mini chocolate chips, white
        decorating icing and colored sugar

1. Preheat oven to 350°F. Line 24 standard (2½-inch) muffin cups with paper baking cups. Spray 24 mini (1¾-inch) muffin cups with nonstick cooking spray. Pat cherries dry with paper towels. Place in food processor; process 4 to 5 seconds or until finely chopped.

2. Beat cake mix, sour cream, oil, egg whites, water and almond extract in large bowl with electric mixer at low speed about 1 minute or until blended. Beat at medium speed 1 to 2 minutes or until smooth. Stir in cherries.

3. Spoon about 2 slightly rounded tablespoons batter into each prepared standard muffin cup, filling about half full. (Cups will be slightly less full than normal.) Spoon remaining batter into prepared mini muffin cups, filling about one-third full.

4. Bake standard cupcakes 14 to 18 minutes and mini cupcakes 7 to 9 minutes or until toothpick inserted into centers comes out clean. Cool cupcakes in pans on wire racks 5 minutes. Remove from pans; cool completely on wire racks.

5. Add food coloring to frosting, a few drops at a time, until desired shade of pink is reached. Frost tops of standard cupcakes. Press top of mini cupcake onto one side of each standard cupcake. Frost mini cupcakes.

6. Place gumdrops between two layers of waxed paper. Flatten to ⅛-inch thickness with rolling pin; cut out triangles. Arrange triangles on cupcakes for ears; complete faces with candy-coated chocolate pieces, chocolate chips, white icing and colored sugar.   *Makes 24 cupcakes*

Miss Pinky the Pig Cupcakes

Doodle Bug Cupcakes

**1 package (about 18 ounces) white cake mix *without* pudding
    in the mix**
1 cup sour cream
3 eggs
⅓ cup water
⅓ cup vegetable oil
1 teaspoon vanilla
1½ cups prepared cream cheese frosting
   Red, yellow, blue and green food coloring
   Red licorice strings, cut into 2-inch pieces
   Assorted round decorating candies

1. Preheat oven to 350°F. Line 24 standard (2½-inch) muffin cups with paper baking cups.

2. Beat cake mix, sour cream, eggs, water, oil and vanilla in large bowl with electric mixer at low speed about 1 minute or until blended. Beat at medium speed 1 to 2 minutes or until smooth. Spoon batter into prepared muffin cups, filling about two-thirds full.

3. Bake about 20 minutes or until toothpick inserted into centers comes out clean. Cool cupcakes in pans on wire racks 5 minutes. Remove from pans; cool completely on wire racks.

4. Divide frosting evenly among 4 small bowls. Add food coloring to each bowl, one drop at a time, until desired shades are reached. Frost tops of cupcakes.

5. Poke three small holes with toothpick on opposite sides of each cupcake, making six holes total. Insert licorice piece into each hole for legs. Decorate cupcakes with assorted candies.   *Makes 24 cupcakes*

Doodle Bug Cupcakes

Play Ball

2 cups plus 1 tablespoon all-purpose flour, divided
¾ cup granulated sugar
¾ cup packed brown sugar
1 tablespoon baking powder
1 teaspoon salt
½ teaspoon baking soda
1¼ cups milk
3 eggs
½ cup shortening
1½ teaspoons vanilla
½ cup mini semisweet chocolate chips
1 container (16 ounces) vanilla frosting
Assorted candies and food colorings

1. Preheat oven to 350°F. Line 24 standard (2½-inch) muffin cups with paper baking cups.

2. Combine 2 cups flour, granulated sugar, brown sugar, baking powder, salt and baking soda in medium bowl. Beat milk, eggs, shortening and vanilla in large bowl with electric mixer at medium speed until well blended. Add flour mixture; beat at high speed 4 minutes, scraping side of bowl frequently.

3. Toss chocolate chips with remaining 1 tablespoon flour in small bowl; stir into batter. Spoon batter evenly into prepared muffin cups.

4. Bake 20 minutes or until toothpick inserted into centers comes out clean. Cool cupcakes in pans on wire racks 5 minutes. Remove from pans; cool completely on wire racks.

5. Decorate with frosting and candies to resemble baseballs, basketballs and soccer balls. *Makes 24 cupcakes*

Holiday Fun

Chocolate Sweetheart Cupcakes

**1 package (about 18 ounces) dark chocolate cake mix,
plus ingredients to prepare mix**
1 container (16 ounces) vanilla frosting
3 tablespoons seedless raspberry jam

1. Preheat oven to 350°F. Line 24 standard (2½-inch) muffin cups with paper baking cups.

2. Prepare cake mix according to package directions. Spoon batter into prepared muffin cups, filling two-thirds full.

3. Bake about 18 minutes or until toothpick inserted into centers comes out clean. Cool cupcakes in pans on wire racks 10 minutes. Remove from pans; cool completely on wire racks.

4. Blend frosting and jam in medium bowl until smooth. Cut off rounded tops of cupcakes with serrated knife. Cut out heart shape from each cupcake top with mini cookie cutter; reserve cutouts.

5. Spread frosting mixture generously over cupcake bottoms, mounding slightly in center. Replace cupcake tops, pressing gently to fill hearts with frosting mixture. Garnish with cutouts; sprinkle with powdered sugar, if desired.

Makes 24 cupcakes

Clockwise from top left: Chocolate Sweetheart Cupcake, Luck o' the Irish Cupcakes (page 114), Easy Easter Cupcakes (page 116) and Boo Hands Cupcakes (page 123)

I Think You're "Marbleous" Cupcakes

**1 package (about 18 ounces) cake mix, any flavor, with pudding
   in mix**
1¼ cups water
3 eggs
¼ cup vegetable oil
1 container (16 ounces) vanilla frosting
1 tube (4¼ ounces) red decorating gel

1. Preheat oven to 350°F. Grease 24 standard (2½-inch) muffin cups or line with paper baking cups.

2. Prepare cake mix according to package directions with water, eggs and oil. Spoon batter into prepared muffin cups, filling two-thirds full.

3. Bake 20 to 25 minutes or until toothpick inserted into centers comes out clean. Cool cupcakes in pans on wire racks 20 minutes. Remove from pans; cool completely on wire racks.

4. Spread 1½ to 2 tablespoons frosting over each cupcake. Fit round decorating tip onto tube of icing. Squeeze 5 dots of icing over each cupcake. Swirl toothpick through icing and frosting in continuous motion to make marbleized pattern or heart shapes.   *Makes 24 cupcakes*

Angelic Cupcakes

1 package (about 16 ounces) angel food cake mix
1¼ cups cold water
¼ teaspoon peppermint extract (optional)
   Red food coloring
4½ cups whipped topping
   Colored sugar and decors (optional)

1. Preheat oven to 375°F. Line 36 standard (2½-inch) muffin cups with paper baking cups.

2. Beat cake mix, water and peppermint extract, if desired, in large bowl with electric mixer at low speed 2 minutes. Pour half of batter into medium bowl; fold in 9 drops red food coloring. Alternate spoonfuls of white and pink batter in each prepared muffin cup, filling about three-fourths full.

continued on page 112

Angelic Cupcakes, continued

3. Bake 11 minutes or until cupcakes are golden brown with deep cracks on top. Remove from pans; cool completely on wire racks.

4. Divide whipped topping between two small bowls. Add 2 drops red food coloring to one bowl of whipped topping; stir gently to blend. Frost cupcakes with pink and white whipped topping; decorate as desired. Refrigerate leftovers.   *Makes 36 cupcakes*

Variation: These pink cupcakes are perfect for Valentine's Day, but you can change the color to match the occasion—pastel pink and purple cupcakes make simple and elegant desserts for baby and bridal showers.

Pretty-in-Pink Peppermint Cupcakes

   1 package (about 18 ounces) white cake mix
1⅓ cups water
   3 egg whites
   2 tablespoons vegetable oil or melted butter
  ½ teaspoon peppermint extract
   3 to 4 drops red liquid food coloring *or* ¼ teaspoon gel food coloring
   1 container (16 ounces) prepared vanilla frosting
  ½ cup crushed peppermint candies (about 16 candies)

1. Preheat oven to 350°F. Line 30 standard (2½-inch) muffin cups with paper baking cups.

2. Beat cake mix, water, egg whites, oil, peppermint extract and food coloring in large bowl with electric mixer at low speed 30 seconds. Beat at medium speed 2 minutes. Spoon batter into prepared muffin cups, filling three-fourths full.

3. Bake 20 to 22 minutes or until toothpick inserted into centers comes out clean. Cool cupcakes in pans on wire racks 10 minutes. Remove from pans; cool completely on wire racks.

4. Frost cupcakes; sprinkle with crushed candies. Store at room temperature up to 24 hours or cover and refrigerate up to 3 days.

Makes 30 cupcakes

Pretty-in-Pink Peppermint Cupcakes

Leprechaun Cupcakes

**1 package (about 18 ounces) yellow or white cake mix, plus
   ingredients to prepare mix**
1 container (16 ounces) vanilla frosting
   **Green, orange and red gumdrops, black decorating gel and
   small candies**

1. Preheat oven to 350°F. Line 24 (2½-inch) muffin cups with paper baking
cups.

2. Prepare cake mix according to package directions. Spoon batter into
prepared muffin cups, filling two-thirds full.

3. Bake 15 to 20 minutes or until toothpick inserted into centers comes out
clean. Cool cupcakes in pans on wire racks 10 minutes. Remove from pans;
cool completely on wire racks. Frost cupcakes with vanilla frosting.

4. Roll out green gumdrops on generously sugared surface. Cut out pieces to
resemble hats. Pipe gel onto hats for hatbands; place candies on hatbands for
buckles. Place hats on cupcakes. Roll out orange gumdrops on generously
sugared surface. Cut out pieces to resemble sideburns and beards; place
on cupcakes. Roll out red gumdrops on generously sugared surface. Cut
out small pieces to resemble mouths; place on cupcakes. Place candies on
cupcakes for eyes.   *Makes 24 cupcakes*

Luck o' the Irish Cupcakes

**1 package (about 18 ounces) cake mix, any flavor, plus ingredients
   to prepare mix**
1 container (16 ounces) white frosting
1 tube (4¼ ounces) green decorating icing
   Green and orange sprinkles, decors and colored sugar

1. Preheat oven to 350°F. Line 24 standard (2½-inch) muffin cups with
paper baking cups.

2. Prepare cake mix according to package directions. Spoon batter into
prepared muffin cups, filling two-thirds full.

3. Bake 15 to 20 minutes or until toothpick inserted into centers comes
out clean. Cool cupcakes in pans on wire racks 10 minutes. Remove from
pans; cool completely on wire racks. Frost cupcakes. Use icing to pipe Irish
phrases or shamrock designs onto cupcakes. Decorate with sprinkles, decors
and colored sugar as desired.   *Makes 24 cupcakes*

Easter Baskets and Bunnies Cupcakes

   2 cups sugar
1¾ cups all-purpose flour
   ¾ cup HERSHEY'S Cocoa or HERSHEY'S SPECIAL DARK™ Cocoa
1½ teaspoons baking powder
1½ teaspoons baking soda
   1 teaspoon salt
   2 eggs
   1 cup milk
  ½ cup vegetable oil
   2 teaspoons vanilla extract
   1 cup boiling water
     Creamy Vanilla Frosting (recipe follows)
     Green, red and yellow food color
3¾ cups MOUNDS® Sweetened Coconut Flakes, divided and tinted*
     Suggested garnishes (marshmallows, HERSHEY'S MINI
       KISSES®ʙʀᴀɴᴅ Milk Chocolates, licorice, jelly beans)

To tint coconut, combine ¾ teaspoon water with several drops green food color in small bowl. Stir in 1¼ cups coconut. Toss with fork until evenly tinted. Repeat with red and yellow food color and remaining coconut.

1. Heat oven to 350°F. Line muffin cups (2½ inches in diameter) with paper bake cups.

2. Stir together sugar, flour, cocoa, baking powder, baking soda and salt in large bowl. Add eggs, milk, oil and vanilla; beat on medium speed of mixer 2 minutes. Stir in boiling water (batter will be thin). Fill muffin cups ⅔ full with batter.

3. Bake 22 to 25 minutes or until wooden pick inserted in center comes out clean. Cool completely. Prepare Creamy Vanilla Frosting; frost cupcakes. Immediately press desired color tinted coconut onto each cupcake. Garnish as desired to resemble Easter basket or bunny.

Makes about 33 cupcakes

Creamy Vanilla Frosting: Beat ⅓ cup softened butter or margarine in medium bowl. Add 1 cup powdered sugar and 1½ teaspoons vanilla extract; beat well. Add 2½ cups powdered sugar alternately with ¼ cup milk, beating to spreading consistency. Makes about 2 cups frosting.

Easy Easter Cupcakes

**1 package (about 18 ounces) yellow cake mix, plus ingredients
   to prepare mix**
1 container (16 ounces) vanilla frosting
   Green food coloring
24 colored sugar-coated marshmallow chicks and/or rabbits
   Assorted white candies

1. Preheat oven to 350°F. Line 24 standard (2½-inch) muffin cups with paper baking cups.

2. Prepare cake mix and bake in prepared muffin cups according to package directions for cupcakes. Cool cupcakes in pans on wire racks 10 minutes. Remove from pans; cool completely on wire racks.

3. Add food coloring to frosting, a few drops at a time, until desired shade of green is reached. Frost cupcakes.

4. Trim marshmallow animals with scissors or knife to fit on cupcakes. Arrange marshmallows on frosting; decorate edges of cupcakes with white candies.   *Makes 24 cupcakes*

Helpful Hint

*When stored tightly sealed in a cool,
dry place, liquid food coloring will last
four years and paste colors will last indefinitely.*

Easy Easter Cupcakes

Spider Cupcakes

1 package (about 18 ounces) yellow or white cake mix
1 cup solid-pack pumpkin
¾ cup water
3 eggs
2 tablespoons vegetable oil
1 teaspoon ground cinnamon
1 teaspoon pumpkin pie spice*
  Orange food coloring
1 container (16 ounces) vanilla, cream cheese or caramel frosting
4 squares (1 ounce each) semisweet chocolate
48 black gumdrops

Or substitute ½ teaspoon ground cinnamon, ¼ teaspoon ground ginger and ⅛ teaspoon each ground allspice and ground nutmeg.

1. Preheat oven to 350°F. Line 24 standard (2½-inch) muffin cups with paper baking cups or spray with nonstick cooking spray.

2. Beat cake mix, pumpkin, water, eggs, oil, cinnamon and pumpkin pie spice in large bowl with electric mixer at medium speed 3 minutes or until well blended.

3. Spoon ¼ cup batter into each prepared muffin cup. Bake about 20 minutes or until toothpick inserted into centers comes out clean. Cool cupcakes in pans 10 minutes. Remove from pans; cool completely on wire racks.

4. Add food coloring to frosting until desired shade of orange is reached. Frost cupcakes. Place chocolate in small resealable food storage bag. Microwave on MEDIUM (50%) 40 seconds. Knead bag; microwave 30 seconds to 1 minute or until chocolate is melted. Knead bag until chocolate is smooth. Cut off tiny corner of bag. Drizzle chocolate in four or five concentric circles over top of cupcakes. Immediately draw 6 to 8 lines at regular intervals from center to edges of cupcakes with toothpick or knife to create web.

5. For spiders, place one gumdrop in center of web. Roll out another gumdrop with rolling pin on generously sugared surface. Slice thinly and roll into "legs." Arrange legs around gumdrop to create spiders.

Makes 24 cupcakes

Spider Cupcakes

Little Devils

1 package (about 18 ounces) carrot cake mix
3 eggs
½ cup solid-pack pumpkin
⅓ cup vegetable oil
1 container (16 ounces) cream cheese frosting
   Assorted Halloween candies, jelly beans, chocolate candies and nuts

1. Preheat oven to 350°F. Line 18 standard (2½-inch) muffin cups with paper baking cups.

2. Prepare cake mix according to package directions, using water as directed on package, eggs, pumpkin and oil. Spoon batter evenly into prepared muffin cups.

3. Bake 20 minutes or until toothpick inserted into centers comes out clean. Cool cupcakes in pans on wire racks 5 minutes. Remove from pans; cool completely on wire racks.

4. Frost cupcakes; decorate with assorted candies.   *Makes 18 cupcakes*

Black Cat Cupcakes

1 package (about 18 ounces) cake mix, any flavor, plus ingredients to
      prepare mix
1 container (16 ounces) chocolate fudge frosting
   Graham crackers
   Black string licorice
   Assorted candies

1. Preheat oven to 350°F. Line 24 standard (2½-inch) muffin cups with paper baking cups.

2. Prepare cake mix according to package directions. Spoon batter into prepared muffin cups, filling two-thirds full.

3. Bake 15 to 20 minutes or until toothpick inserted into centers comes out clean. Cool cupcakes in pans on wire racks 10 minutes. Remove from pans; cool completely on wire racks.

4. Frost cupcakes. Cut graham crackers into small triangles with serrated knife; place on cupcakes to form ears. Decorate faces with licorice and assorted candies.   *Makes 24 cupcakes*

Little Devils

Scarecrow Cupcakes

1¼ cups all-purpose flour
¾ teaspoon baking powder
¾ teaspoon ground cinnamon
½ teaspoon baking soda
¼ teaspoon salt
⅛ teaspoon ground nutmeg
⅛ teaspoon ground cloves
⅛ teaspoon ground allspice
¾ cup whipping cream
2 tablespoons molasses
¼ cup (½ stick) butter, softened
¼ cup granulated sugar
¼ cup packed brown sugar
2 eggs
½ teaspoon vanilla
¾ cup sweetened shredded coconut
   Maple Frosting (recipe follows)
   Toasted coconut, chow mein noodles, shredded wheat cereal,
      assorted candies and decorating gel

1. Preheat oven to 350°F. Line 18 standard (2½-inch) muffin cups with paper baking cups. Combine flour, baking powder, cinnamon, baking soda, salt, nutmeg, cloves and allspice in medium bowl. Combine cream and molasses in small bowl.

2. Beat butter in large bowl until creamy. Add granulated sugar and brown sugar; beat until light and fluffy. Add eggs, one at a time, beating well after each addition. Beat in vanilla. Add flour mixture alternately with cream mixture, beating well after each addition. Stir in coconut. Spoon batter into prepared muffin cups, filling about half full.

3. Bake 20 to 25 minutes or until toothpick inserted into centers comes out clean. Cool cupcakes in pans on wire racks 10 minutes. Remove from pans; cool completely on wire racks.

4. Prepare Maple Frosting. Frost cupcakes and decorate to create scarecrow faces.   *Makes 18 cupcakes*

Maple Frosting: Beat 2 tablespoons softened butter and 2 tablespoons maple syrup in medium bowl until well blended. Gradually beat in 1½ cups powdered sugar until smooth.

Tip: To make a gumdrop hat, roll out a large gumdrop on a generously sugared surface. Cut 1 rounded piece for the top of the hat and 1 straight piece for the brim. Overlap the pieces to make the hat; pipe decorator gel over the seam for the hat band.

Boo Hands Cupcakes

1 package (about 18 ounces) cake mix, any flavor, plus ingredients to prepare mix
1 container (16 ounces) white frosting
36 large marshmallows
24 black jelly beans, halved
12 orange jelly beans, halved

1. Preheat oven to 350°F. Line 24 standard (2½-inch) muffin cups with paper baking cups or spray with nonstick cooking spray.

2. Prepare cake mix according to package directions. Spoon batter evenly into prepared muffin cups.

3. Bake 15 to 20 minutes or until toothpick inserted into centers comes out clean. Cool cupcakes in pans on wire racks 15 minutes. Remove from pans; cool completely on wire racks.

4. Spread small amount of frosting on cupcakes. Cut 12 marshmallows in half crosswise; place one half on each cupcake. Frost cupcakes again, completely covering marshmallow half.

5. Roll remaining marshmallows between hands until about 2½ inches long. Cut in half and arrange on either side of cupcakes to create hands; cover completely with frosting. Create faces with black jelly bean halves for eyes and orange jelly bean half for nose.   *Makes 24 cupcakes*

Magical Wizard Hats

**1 package (about 18 ounces) cake mix, any flavor, plus ingredients
    to prepare mix**
2 containers (16 ounces each) vanilla frosting
   Yellow and purple or black food coloring
2 packages (4 ounces each) sugar cones
   Orange sugar
   Decors
   Black decorating gel

1. Preheat oven to 350°F. Line 24 standard (2½-inch) muffin cups with paper baking cups or spray with nonstick cooking spray.

2. Prepare cake mix and bake in prepared muffin cups according to package directions for cupcakes. Cool cupcakes in pans on wire racks 15 minutes. Remove from pans; cool completely on wire racks.

3. Frost cupcakes with one container vanilla frosting. Place ½ cup remaining frosting in small bowl; tint with yellow food coloring. Tint remaining frosting with purple or black food coloring.

4. Spread sugar cones with dark frosting, covering completely. Place one cone upside down on each frosted cupcake. Spoon yellow frosting into small resealable food storage bag. Cut off small corner of bag; pipe yellow frosting around base of each frosted cone. Decorate with sugar, decors and decorating gel.   *Makes 24 cupcakes*

Magical Wizard Hats

Cobweb Cups

**1 package (about 18 ounces) brownie mix, plus ingredients
  to prepare mix**
½ cup mini chocolate chips
2 ounces cream cheese, softened
1 egg
2 tablespoons sugar
2 tablespoons all-purpose flour
¼ teaspoon vanilla

1. Preheat oven to 350°F. Line 18 standard (2½-inch) muffin cups with paper baking cups.

2. Prepare brownie mix according to package directions for cakelike brownies; stir in chocolate chips. Spoon batter evenly into prepared muffin cups.

3. Beat cream cheese and egg in small bowl until well blended. Add sugar, flour and vanilla; beat until well blended and smooth.

4. Place cream cheese mixture in resealable food storage bag; seal bag. Cut off small corner of bag with scissors; pipe cream cheese mixture in concentric circle design on each cupcake. Draw toothpick through cream cheese mixture 6 to 8 times out from center.

5. Bake 20 to 25 minutes or until toothpick inserted into centers comes out clean. Cool cupcakes in pans on wire racks 15 minutes. Remove from pans; cool completely on wire racks. *Makes 18 cupcakes*

Cobweb Cups

Reindeer Cupcakes

1 package (about 18 ounces) chocolate cake mix, plus ingredients
    to prepare mix
¼ cup (½ stick) butter, softened
4 cups powdered sugar
5 to 6 tablespoons brewed espresso, divided
½ cup (3 ounces) semisweet chocolate chips, melted
1 teaspoon vanilla
   Dash salt
24 pretzel twists, broken in half
   Assorted candies

1. Preheat oven to 350°F. Line 24 standard (2½-inch) muffin cups with paper baking cups.

2. Prepare cake mix according to package directions. Spoon batter into prepared muffin cups, filling two-thirds full.

3. Bake 15 to 20 minutes or until toothpick inserted into centers comes out clean. Cool cupcakes in pans on wire racks 10 minutes. Remove from pans; cool completely on wire racks.

4. Beat butter in large bowl with electric mixer at medium speed until creamy. Gradually add powdered sugar and 4 tablespoons espresso; beat until smooth. Add melted chocolate, vanilla and salt; beat until well blended. Add remaining espresso, 1 tablespoon at a time, until frosting is of desired spreading consistency.

5. Frost cupcakes. Decorate with broken pretzel pieces for antlers and assorted candies for faces.   *Makes 24 cupcakes*

Reindeer Cupcakes

TREE TRIMMING
PARTY

Cupcakes for Breakfast

Spiced Orange Cranberry Muffins

½ **cup chopped cranberries**
3 **tablespoons packed brown sugar**
1 **cup orange juice**
1 **egg white**
2 **tablespoons canola or vegetable oil**
1 **cup whole wheat flour**
½ **cup all-purpose flour**
1½ **teaspoons baking powder**
½ **teaspoon ground cinnamon**
¼ **teaspoon ground nutmeg**

1. Preheat oven to 400°F. Line 8 standard (2¾-inch) muffin cups or spray with nonstick cooking spray.

2. Combine cranberries and sugar in medium bowl; let stand 5 minutes. Stir in orange juice, egg white and oil. Combine whole wheat flour, all-purpose flour, baking powder, cinnamon and nutmeg in large bowl. Add cranberry mixture to flour mixture; stir just until moistened. Spoon batter into prepared muffin cups, filling three-fourths full.

3. Bake 18 to 20 minutes or until toothpick inserted into centers comes out clean. Remove muffins from pan; cool on wire rack.   *Makes 8 muffins*

Clockwise from top left: Spiced Orange Cranberry Muffins, Lemon Poppy Seed Muffins (page 142), Double Chocolate Zucchini Muffin (page 144) and Piña Colada Muffins (page 150)

Give Me S'more Muffins

2 cups graham cracker crumbs
⅓ cup sugar
⅓ cup mini chocolate chips
2 teaspoons baking powder
¾ cup milk
1 egg
24 milk chocolate candy kisses, unwrapped
2 cups mini marshmallows

1. Preheat oven to 350°F. Line 24 mini (1¾-inch) muffin cups with foil or paper baking cups.

2. Combine graham cracker crumbs, sugar, chocolate chips and baking powder in medium bowl. Whisk milk and egg in small bowl; stir into crumb mixture until well blended.

3. Spoon batter into prepared muffin cups, filling about half full. Press chocolate kiss into each cup. Press 4 marshmallows into top of each muffin.

4. Bake 10 to 12 minutes or until marshmallows are lightly browned. Cool muffins in pans on wire racks 10 minutes. Remove from pans; cool on wire racks. *Makes 24 mini muffins*

Golden Oatmeal Muffins

1 package DUNCAN HINES® Moist Deluxe® Butter Recipe
    Golden Cake Mix
1 cup uncooked quick-cooking oats (not instant or old-fashioned)
¼ teaspoon salt
¾ cup milk
2 eggs, lightly beaten
2 tablespoons butter or margarine, melted

1. Preheat oven to 400°F. Grease 24 (2½-inch) muffin cups (or use paper liners).

2. Combine cake mix, oats and salt in large bowl. Add milk, eggs and melted butter; stir until moistened. Fill muffin cups two-thirds full. Bake at 400°F for 13 minutes or until golden brown. Cool in pan 5 to 10 minutes. Loosen carefully before removing from pan. Serve with honey or your favorite jam. *Makes 2 dozen muffins*

Give Me S'more Muffins

Banana Peanut Butter Chip Muffins

  2 cups all-purpose flour
  ¾ cup sugar
  2 teaspoons baking powder
  ½ teaspoon baking soda
  ¼ teaspoon salt
  1 cup mashed ripe bananas (about 2 large)
  ½ cup (1 stick) butter, melted
  2 eggs, beaten
  ⅓ cup buttermilk
1½ teaspoons vanilla
  1 cup peanut butter chips
  ½ cup chopped peanuts

1. Preheat oven to 375°F. Grease 15 standard (2½-inch) muffins cups or line with paper baking cups.

2. Combine flour, sugar, baking powder, baking soda and salt in large bowl. Beat bananas, butter, eggs, buttermilk and vanilla in medium bowl until well blended.

3. Add banana mixture to flour mixture; stir just until blended. Gently fold in peanut butter chips. Spoon batter into prepared muffin cups, filling three-fourths full. Sprinkle with peanuts.

4. Bake 20 minutes or until toothpick inserted into centers comes out clean. Cool muffins in pans 2 minutes. Remove from pans; cool on wire racks. Serve warm or at room temperature. *Makes 15 muffins*

Helpful Hint

Substitute a mixture of chocolate and peanut butter chips in place of the peanut butter chips for a combination of three great flavors in one muffin.

Banana Peanut Butter Chip Muffins

Mixed-Up Muffins

2 cups all-purpose flour
1 cup sugar, divided
2 teaspoons baking powder
½ teaspoon baking soda
¼ teaspoon salt
⅓ cup mini chocolate chips
⅓ cup unsweetened cocoa powder
1¼ cups milk
2 eggs
⅓ cup vegetable oil
1 teaspoon vanilla

1. Preheat oven to 400°F. Line 15 standard (2½-inch) muffin cups with paper baking cups or spray with nonstick cooking spray.

2. Combine flour, ¾ cup sugar, baking powder, baking soda and salt in medium bowl. Remove 1½ cups mixture to separate medium bowl; stir in chocolate chips. Stir cocoa and remaining ¼ cup sugar into remaining flour mixture.

3. Beat milk, eggs, oil and vanilla in another medium bowl. Add half of milk mixture to each bowl of dry ingredients. Stir each batter separately just until moistened. Spoon white and chocolate batters side by side into prepared muffin cups, filling about three-fourths full.

4. Bake 20 to 25 minutes or until toothpick inserted into centers comes out clean. Cool muffins in pans on wire racks 2 minutes. Serve warm or at room temperature.   *Makes 15 muffins*

Mixed-Up Muffins

Cocoa Orange Muffins

2 cups all-purpose flour
¾ cup sugar
¼ cup HERSHEY₃S Cocoa
1 tablespoon baking powder
⅔ cup milk
¼ cup orange juice
¼ cup vegetable oil
1 egg
1 tablespoon freshly grated orange peel
Orange Sugar Topping (recipe follows)

1. Heat oven to 400°F. Grease or line twelve muffin cups (2½ inches in diameter) with paper bake cups.

2. Stir together flour, sugar, cocoa and baking powder in large bowl. Stir together milk, orange juice, oil, egg and orange peel in small bowl; add to dry ingredients, stirring just until moistened. Fill muffin cups ¾ full with batter. Sprinkle Orange Sugar Topping over muffins.

3. Bake 20 minutes or until wooden pick inserted in center comes out clean. Serve warm.   *Makes 1 dozen muffins*

Orange Sugar Topping: Mix together 2 tablespoons sugar and 1½ teaspoons finely grated orange peel.

Cranberry Cheesecake Muffins

1 package (3 ounces) cream cheese, softened
4 tablespoons sugar, divided
1 cup milk
⅓ cup vegetable oil
1 egg
1 package (about 15 ounces) cranberry quick bread mix

1. Preheat oven to 400°F. Grease 12 standard (2½-inch) muffin cups.

2. Beat cream cheese and 2 tablespoons sugar in small bowl until well blended. Beat milk, oil and egg in large bowl until blended. Stir in quick bread mix just until moistened.

3. Spoon batter into prepared muffin cups, filling one-fourth full. Drop 1 teaspoon cream cheese mixture into center of each cup. Top with remaining batter. Sprinkle with remaining 2 tablespoons sugar.

4. Bake 17 to 22 minutes or until golden brown. Cool muffins in pan on wire rack 5 minutes. Remove from pan; cool completely on wire rack.

Makes 12 muffins

Maple Magic Muffins

½ **cup plus 3 tablespoons maple syrup,* divided**
¼ **cup chopped walnuts**
 2 **tablespoons butter, melted**
 2 **cups all-purpose flour**
¾ **cup sugar**
 2 **teaspoons baking powder**
½ **teaspoon baking soda**
½ **teaspoon salt**
¼ **teaspoon cinnamon**
¾ **cup plus 1 tablespoon milk**
½ **cup vegetable oil**
 1 **egg**
½ **teaspoon vanilla**

*For best flavor and texture, use pure maple syrup, not pancake syrup.

1. Preheat oven to 400°F. Grease 12 standard (2½-inch) muffin cups, preferably nonstick. Place 2 teaspoons maple syrup, 1 teaspoon walnuts and ½ teaspoon melted butter in each cup.

2. Combine flour, sugar, baking powder, baking soda, salt and cinnamon in large bowl; mix well. Whisk milk, oil, egg, remaining 3 tablespoons maple syrup and vanilla in medium bowl until well blended. Add to flour mixture; stir just until blended. Spoon batter into prepared muffin cups, filling two-thirds full. Place muffin pan on baking sheet to catch any drips (maple syrup may overflow slightly).

3. Bake 20 to 25 minutes or until toothpick inserted into centers comes out clean. Invert pan onto wire rack covered with waxed paper. Cool muffins slightly; serve warm.

Makes 12 muffins

Apricot Mini Muffins

1½ cups all-purpose flour
½ cup sugar
½ cup finely chopped dried apricots
¼ teaspoon baking powder
¼ teaspoon baking soda
⅛ teaspoon salt
   Pinch ground nutmeg
½ cup (1 stick) butter, melted and cooled to room temperature
2 eggs
2 tablespoons milk
1 teaspoon vanilla

1. Preheat oven to 350°F. Spray 24 mini (1¾-inch) muffin cups with nonstick cooking spray.

2. Combine flour, sugar, apricots, baking powder, baking soda, salt and nutmeg in large bowl; mix well. Whisk butter, eggs, milk and vanilla in medium bowl. Add butter mixture to flour mixture; mix just until moistened. Spoon about 1 tablespoon batter into each prepared muffin cup.

3. Bake 12 to 15 minutes or until toothpick inserted into centers comes out clean. Cool muffins in pans on wire rack 5 minutes. Remove from pans; cool completely on wire racks.   *Makes 24 mini muffins*

Apricot Mini Muffins

Lemon Poppy Seed Muffins

　2 cups all-purpose flour
1¼ cups granulated sugar
　¼ cup poppy seeds
　2 tablespoons plus 2 teaspoons grated lemon peel, divided
　2 teaspoons baking powder
　½ teaspoon baking soda
　½ teaspoon ground cardamom
　¼ teaspoon salt
　2 eggs
　½ cup (1 stick) butter, melted
　½ cup milk
　½ cup plus 2 tablespoons lemon juice, divided
　1 cup powdered sugar

1. Preheat oven to 400°F. Line 18 standard (2½-inch) muffin cups with paper baking cups or spray with nonstick cooking spray.

2. Combine flour, granulated sugar, poppy seeds, 2 tablespoons lemon peel, baking powder, baking soda, cardamom and salt in large bowl. Beat eggs in medium bowl. Add butter, milk and ½ cup lemon juice; mix well. Add egg mixture to flour mixture; stir just until moistened. Spoon batter into prepared muffin cups, filling three-fourths full.

3. Bake 15 to 20 minutes or until toothpick inserted into centers comes out clean. Cool muffins in pans on wire racks 10 minutes.

4. Meanwhile, prepare glaze. Combine powdered sugar and remaining 2 teaspoons lemon peel in small bowl; stir in enough remaining lemon juice to make pourable glaze. Place muffins on sheet of foil or waxed paper; drizzle with glaze. Serve warm or at room temperature.

Makes 18 muffins

Lemon Poppy Seed Muffins

Double Chocolate Zucchini Muffins

2⅓ cups all-purpose flour
1¼ cups sugar
⅓ cup unsweetened cocoa powder
2 teaspoons baking powder
1½ teaspoons ground cinnamon
1 teaspoon baking soda
½ teaspoon salt
1 cup sour cream
½ cup vegetable oil
2 eggs, beaten
¼ cup milk
1 cup milk chocolate chips
1 cup shredded zucchini

1. Preheat oven to 400°F. Line 12 jumbo (3½-inch) muffin cups with paper baking cups or spray with nonstick cooking spray.

2. Combine flour, sugar, cocoa, baking powder, cinnamon, baking soda and salt in large bowl. Combine sour cream, oil, eggs and milk in medium bowl until blended; stir into flour mixture just until moistened. Fold in chocolate chips and zucchini. Spoon batter into prepared muffin cups, filling half full.

3. Bake 25 to 30 minutes or until toothpick inserted into centers comes out clean. Cool muffins in pan on wire rack 5 minutes. Remove from pan; cool completely on wire rack. Store tightly covered at room temperature.

Makes 12 jumbo muffins

Variation: For standard-size muffins, spoon batter into 18 standard (2½-inch) paper-lined or greased muffin cups. Bake at 400°F 18 to 20 minutes or until toothpick inserted into centers comes out clean.

Double Chocolate Zucchini Muffins

Honey Pumpkin Muffins

¼ **cup butter or margarine, softened**
¾ **cup honey**
1 **egg**
1 **cup solid-pack pumpkin**
1½ **cups all-purpose flour**
1½ **teaspoons baking powder**
1 **teaspoon baking soda**
¼ **teaspoon salt**
1 **cup chopped toasted walnuts**

Using electric mixer, beat butter until light; gradually add honey, beating until light and creamy. Beat in egg and pumpkin.

In medium bowl, combine flour, baking powder, baking soda and salt. Gradually add to butter mixture, mixing until blended; stir in walnuts. Spoon batter into 12 greased or paper-lined 2½-inch muffin cups. Bake at 350°F for 25 to 30 minutes or until toothpick inserted in center comes out clean. Remove muffins from pan; cool on wire rack.   *Makes 12 muffins*

*Favorite recipe from **National Honey Board***

StrawBabies

2 **cups all-purpose flour**
¾ **cup sugar**
2 **teaspoons baking powder**
¾ **teaspoon baking soda**
¾ **teaspoon salt**
1 **cup coarsely chopped fresh strawberries (about 1 pint)**
1 **container (6 ounces) strawberry yogurt (blended, not fruit
   at the bottom)**
¾ **cup milk**
½ **cup vegetable oil**
1 **egg**
¼ **teaspoon almond extract**

1. Preheat oven to 400°F. Grease 36 mini (1¾-inch) muffin cups or line with paper baking cups.

146

2. Combine flour, sugar, baking powder, baking soda and salt in large bowl. Add strawberries; toss until evenly coated. Beat yogurt, milk, oil, egg and almond extract in medium bowl until well blended. Add to flour mixture; stir gently just until moistened. Spoon batter evenly into prepared muffin cups, filling almost full.

3. Bake 10 to 12 minutes or until toothpick inserted into centers comes out clean. Cool muffins in pans on wire racks 2 minutes. Serve warm or at room temperature. *Makes 36 mini muffins*

Apple Raisin Walnut Muffins

>   2 cups all-purpose flour
> ¾ cup sugar
>   2 teaspoons baking powder
>   1 teaspoon ground cinnamon
> ½ teaspoon baking soda
> ½ teaspoon salt
> ¼ teaspoon ground nutmeg
> ¾ cup plus 2 tablespoons milk
>   2 eggs, beaten
> ⅓ cup butter, melted
>   1 cup chopped dried apples
> ½ cup golden raisins
> ½ cup chopped walnuts

1. Preheat oven to 350°F. Grease 6 jumbo (3½-inch) muffin cups.

2. Combine flour, sugar, baking powder, cinnamon, baking soda, salt and nutmeg in large bowl. Beat milk, eggs and butter in small bowl until well blended. Stir into flour mixture just until moistened. Gently fold in apples, raisins and walnuts. Spoon batter into prepared muffin cups, filling three-fourths full.

3. Bake 25 to 30 minutes or until toothpick inserted into centers comes out clean. Cool muffins in pan on wire rack 2 minutes. Serve warm or at room temperature. *Makes 6 jumbo muffins*

Blueberry Crisp Cupcakes

Cupcakes
- **2 cups all-purpose flour**
- **2 teaspoons baking powder**
- **¼ teaspoon salt**
- **1¾ cups granulated sugar**
- **½ cup (1 stick) butter, softened**
- **¾ cup milk**
- **1½ teaspoons vanilla**
- **3 egg whites**
- **3 cups fresh or frozen blueberries**

Streusel
- **⅓ cup all-purpose flour**
- **¼ cup uncooked old-fashioned or quick oats**
- **¼ cup packed light brown sugar**
- **½ teaspoon ground cinnamon**
- **¼ cup (½ stick) butter**
- **½ cup chopped walnuts or pecans**

1. Preheat oven to 350°F. Line 30 standard (2½-inch) muffin cups with foil or paper baking cups or lightly spray with nonstick cooking spray.

2. For cupcakes, combine 2 cups flour, baking powder and salt in medium bowl; mix well. Beat granulated sugar and ½ cup butter in large bowl with electric mixer at medium speed 1 minute. Add milk and vanilla; beat at low speed 30 seconds. Gradually add flour mixture; beat at medium speed 2 minutes. Add egg whites; beat 1 minute. Spoon batter into prepared muffin cups, filling half full. Sprinkle blueberries over batter. Bake 10 minutes.

3. Meanwhile, for streusel, combine ⅓ cup flour, oats, brown sugar and cinnamon in small bowl; mix well. Cut in ¼ cup butter with pastry blender or two knives until mixture resembles coarse crumbs. Stir in nuts.

4. Sprinkle streusel over partially baked cupcakes. Return to oven; bake 18 to 20 minutes or until golden brown and toothpick inserted into centers comes out clean. Cool cupcakes in pans on wire racks 10 minutes. Remove from pans; cool completely on wire racks. Cupcakes may be frozen up to 3 months. *Makes 30 cupcakes*

Blueberry Crisp Cupcakes

Piña Colada Muffins

   2 cups all-purpose flour
   ¾ cup sugar
   ½ cup flaked coconut
   2 teaspoons baking powder
   ½ teaspoon baking soda
   ½ teaspoon salt
   2 eggs
   1 cup sour cream
   1 can (8 ounces) crushed pineapple in juice, undrained
   ¼ cup (½ stick) butter, melted
   ⅛ teaspoon coconut extract
      Additional coconut for garnish (optional)

1. Preheat oven to 400°F. Line 18 standard (2½-inch) muffin cups with paper baking cups or spray with nonstick cooking spray.

2. Combine flour, sugar, coconut, baking powder, baking soda and salt in large bowl. Beat eggs in medium bowl. Blend in sour cream, pineapple with juice, butter and coconut extract. Stir into flour mixture just until moistened. Spoon batter into prepared muffin cups, filling three-fourths full.

3. Bake 10 minutes, then sprinkle tops of muffins with additional coconut, if desired. Bake 5 to 10 minutes more (total of 15 to 20 minutes) or until toothpick inserted into centers comes out clean. Cool muffins in pans on wire racks 2 minutes. Serve warm or at room temperature.

Makes 18 muffins

Piña Colada Muffins

Cranberry Pecan Muffins

1¾ cups all-purpose flour
½ cup packed light brown sugar
2½ teaspoons baking powder
½ teaspoon salt
¾ cup milk
¼ cup (½ stick) butter, melted
1 egg, beaten
1 cup chopped fresh cranberries
⅓ cup chopped pecans
1 teaspoon grated lemon peel

1. Preheat oven to 400°F. Grease 36 mini (1¾-inch) muffin cups or line with paper baking cups.

2. Combine flour, brown sugar, baking powder and salt in large bowl. Combine milk, butter and egg in small bowl until blended; stir into flour mixture just until moistened. Fold in cranberries, pecans and lemon peel. Spoon evenly into prepared muffin cups.

3. Bake 15 to 17 minutes or until toothpick inserted into centers comes out clean. Remove muffins from pans; cool on wire racks.

Makes 36 mini muffins

German Chocolate Muffins

3 tablespoons flaked coconut
3 tablespoons packed brown sugar
3 tablespoons chopped pecans
1 package (about 18 ounces) German chocolate cake mix with pudding in the mix, plus ingredients to prepare mix

1. Preheat oven to 400°F. Grease 12 jumbo (3½-inch) muffin cups. Combine coconut, brown sugar and pecans in small bowl until well blended.

2. Prepare cake mix according to package directions, *reducing water by ¼ cup.* Spoon batter into prepared muffin cups, filling half full. Sprinkle evenly with coconut mixture.

3. Bake 20 to 25 minutes or until toothpick inserted into centers comes out clean. Cool muffins in pan on wire rack 5 minutes. Remove from pan; cool on wire rack 10 minutes. *Makes 12 jumbo muffins*

Cranberry Pecan Muffins

Coffee Walnut Chocolate Chip Muffins

½ **cup (1 stick) butter or margarine, softened**
½ **cup granulated sugar**
½ **cup packed light brown sugar**
2 **to 3 tablespoons powdered instant coffee**
2 **teaspoons vanilla extract**
1¾ **cups all-purpose flour**
1 **tablespoon baking powder**
½ **teaspoon salt**
2 **eggs**
⅔ **cup milk**
1½ **cups coarsely chopped walnuts**
¾ **cup HERSHEY'S Semi-Sweet Chocolate Chips**

1. Heat oven to 350°F. Line twelve muffin cups (2½ inches in diameter) with paper bake cups.

2. Beat butter, granulated sugar, brown sugar, instant coffee and vanilla in large bowl until creamy. Stir together flour, baking powder and salt. Beat together eggs and milk; add alternately with flour mixture to butter mixture, stirring just to combine. Stir in walnuts and chocolate chips. Fill muffin cups ½ full with batter.

3. Bake 20 to 25 minutes. Cool 5 minutes; remove from pans to wire rack. Cool completely.   *Makes 12 muffins*

Helpful Hint

Both light and dark brown sugars are moist when fresh but can easily dry out. Adding a slice of apple or bread to the box or bag will help restore moisture.

Acknowledgments

The publisher would like to thank the companies
and organizations listed below for the use of
their recipes and photographs in this publication.

Duncan Hines® and Moist Deluxe® are registered trademarks of
Pinnacle Foods Corp.

The Hershey Company

© Mars, Incorporated 2008

Mott's® is a registered trademark of Mott's, LLP

National Honey Board

Nestlé USA

Index

METRIC CONVERSION CHART

VOLUME MEASUREMENTS (dry)

1/8 teaspoon = 0.5 mL
1/4 teaspoon = 1 mL
1/2 teaspoon = 2 mL
3/4 teaspoon = 4 mL
1 teaspoon = 5 mL
1 tablespoon = 15 mL
2 tablespoons = 30 mL
1/4 cup = 60 mL
1/3 cup = 75 mL
1/2 cup = 125 mL
2/3 cup = 150 mL
3/4 cup = 175 mL
1 cup = 250 mL
2 cups = 1 pint = 500 mL
3 cups = 750 mL
4 cups = 1 quart = 1 L

VOLUME MEASUREMENTS (fluid)

1 fluid ounce (2 tablespoons) = 30 mL
4 fluid ounces (1/2 cup) = 125 mL
8 fluid ounces (1 cup) = 250 mL
12 fluid ounces (1 1/2 cups) = 375 mL
16 fluid ounces (2 cups) = 500 mL

WEIGHTS (mass)

1/2 ounce = 15 g
1 ounce = 30 g
3 ounces = 90 g
4 ounces = 120 g
8 ounces = 225 g
10 ounces = 285 g
12 ounces = 360 g
16 ounces = 1 pound = 450 g

DIMENSIONS

1/16 inch = 2 mm
1/8 inch = 3 mm
1/4 inch = 6 mm
1/2 inch = 1.5 cm
3/4 inch = 2 cm
1 inch = 2.5 cm

OVEN TEMPERATURES

250°F = 120°C
275°F = 140°C
300°F = 150°C
325°F = 160°C
350°F = 180°C
375°F = 190°C
400°F = 200°C
425°F = 220°C
450°F = 230°C

BAKING PAN SIZES

Utensil	Size in Inches/Quarts	Metric Volume	Size in Centimeters
Baking or Cake Pan (square or rectangular)	8×8×2	2 L	20×20×5
	9×9×2	2.5 L	23×23×5
	12×8×2	3 L	30×20×5
	13×9×2	3.5 L	33×23×5
Loaf Pan	8×4×3	1.5 L	20×10×7
	9×5×3	2 L	23×13×7
Round Layer Cake Pan	8×1½	1.2 L	20×4
	9×1½	1.5 L	23×4
Pie Plate	8×1¼	750 mL	20×3
	9×1¼	1 L	23×3
Baking Dish or Casserole	1 quart	1 L	—
	1½ quart	1.5 L	—
	2 quart	2 L	—